PRINCIPAL WORKS OF ALBERTO SAVINIO

FICTION

Hermaphrodito, 1918; *La casa ispirata*, 1925
Angelica o la notte di maggio, 1927
Tragedia dell'infanzia, 1937; *Achille innamorato*, 1938
Infanzia di Nivasio Dolcemare, 1941
Dico a te, Clio, 1941
Ascolto il tuo cuore, città, 1943
Casa "La Vita", 1943; *La nostra anima*, 1944
Tutta la vita, 1945; *L'angolino*, 1950

ESSAYS

Seconda vita di Gemito, 1938; *Leo Longanesi*, 1942
Narrate, uomini, la vostra storia, 1942
Scatola sonora, 1955; *Maupassant e "l'altro"*, 1960

PLAYS

Capitan Ulisse, 1929; *La famiglia Mastinu*, 1948
Emma B. vedova Giocasta, 1949
Alcesti di Samuele, 1949; *Orfeo vedovo*, 1950

Speaking to Clio

Alberto Savinio

Speaking to Clio

Translated by John Shepley

THE MARLBORO PRESS
MARLBORO, VERMONT
1987

Originally published in Italian as
DICO A TE, CLIO

Manufactured in the United States of America

Library of Congress Catalog Card Number 86-63743

Cloth: ISBN 0-910395-22-5
Paper: ISBN 0-910395-23-3

THE MARLBORO PRESS

MARLBORO, VERMONT

AUTHOR'S NOTE

Of the two books now being reissued by the publisher, Sansoni (*Tragedia dell'infanzia* [*Tragedy of Childhood*] is from 1920, *Speaking to Clio* from 1939), the first is a forest, the second a garden. *Tragedia dell'infanzia* is a forest for the darkness that grows thicker in that most murky season of life; *Speaking to Clio* is a garden for the clarity, lightness, and amenity that I acquired in my mature years.

From that story to these journeys, the astute reader will above all be able to measure the passage from a raw dish to a cooked one.

For in *bonae litterae* as well as in cuisine, it's all a matter of cooking.

A. S. (Rome, 1946)

Speaking to Clio

Clio: χλείω: I close. History collects our actions and gradually deposits them in the past. History gradually frees us from the past. A perfect organization of life would ensure that all our actions, even the least and most insignificant, become history, so as to relieve us of them, take them off our backs. The habit of consigning our daily actions to a diary is a rule of hygiene, and the man with an active mind is implicitly a memorialist, who deposits his "inner actions" in his memoirs, that is to say in his works. We ought to get in the habit as children of keeping a diary, just as we get in the habit of brushing our teeth. As for washing our face in the morning, we do it to cleanse it of our dreams, those "actions" of sleep, those nocturnal "sins." That civilization will be perfect that translates everything into history and allows us to rediscover ourselves each morning in a fresh condition, free from the past. What we obtain by history, others obtain by confession, and we call actions what they call sins. Using the same language, we can say that any action is sin, and living, this uninterrupted sequence of actions, is a continual process of sinning. Some also put poetry among the forms of catharsis, saying that poetry frees us from the slavery of passion, but they are wrong. Poetry — and the arts, instruments of poetry — has no relations with passion, but makes use of incorruptible elements that lie beyond passion. Of course, I am here speaking of poetry in its metaphysical quality. The ills of the world, its slowness, its obstacles, its stupidity, can be attributed to the incomplete functioning of history. The past festers on some men and rots. In the proper darkness, they would shine from the filth coating them like a crust. Heaps of "unhistorified" material choke the pathways of the world. This constant throwing of the past over one's shoulder, this constant "self-purification" . . . So does life have an end? In the last gaze coming from our eyes, the last light from our intelligence, that gaze, that light, will not be directed to the past, placed for good behind the closed door, but to the future. And the future, as you will have understood, ladies and gentlemen, is death, inaction par excellence and supreme purity.

The malfunctioning of history is compensated in part by an unwritten history, a non-oral history, a non-mnemonic history, a history "nonhistorical" but a natural and spontaneous catharsis: a "ghost" of history. The absurd axiom, the cruel axiom, the forced axiom that "nothing is lost in nature" has finally been belied. Beyond the murkiest depths, beyond the most unfathomable abysses, our souls will recognize the true goal of life: to disappear. Alongside history, which gradually stops the actions of men, confines them, and makes them inoperative, there is the ghost of history: the great hole, the void that little by little absorbs the actions that escape history and annihilates them. Our extraordinary sight, made extraordinarily acute in an extraordinary moment of our lives, has allowed us for a moment to see once again the annihilated actions inside that void, the deeds that no longer exist, the vanished vicissitudes, the things that no one will ever be able to see again. A very thin garden, in which the ghosts of the flowers were dying. And if the annihilated deeds were the only memorable ones? What if the greatest destiny of human vicissitudes, the noblest, highest, "holiest" fate of ourselves and our thoughts were not history, but the ghost of history?

Arnold Böcklin used to prepare his canvases in gray; then with a sponge soaked in water he would lay out in large masses the composition he had in mind; finally he would sit down and contemplate for a long time this preliminary ghost of his new work. If the damp sketch satisfied him, he would go back over it with paint and fix its outlines; if not, he allowed it little by little to fade away.

Works that enter into history — works that enter into the ghost of history.

Memories, too, slowly but inexorably fade.

That morning Charun, he who escorts souls from this life to the other, awakened me and told me it was time to go. I didn't even think of asking to see his arrest warrant, and followed him without saying a word.

Ari, 12 August 1939

On our host's terrace, at Ari. His name sounds strange outside Abruzzo: it is Concezio. We are in the situation of a painting by Hans von Thoma, the last of the German Romantic painters. In this artist's panoramic landscapes, a figure placed in the foreground looks at the landscape with obvious satisfaction, as though inviting the spectator to do likewise. At Ari, the role of the "decoy" figure is played in the flesh by Concezio. With his finger he traces a slow semicircle over the panorama and says, "Here we are in the Chietino." At the unexpected resonance of this geographical designation, we look at each other in the fear of having misunderstood.

Concezio weighs well over two hundred pounds and is proportionately tall. Other times we had been saddened by the thought that the race of giants had disappeared, but Concezio has brought joy back to our hearts. The day before yesterday, on the beach at the Pineta di Pescara, we saw him in a bathing suit: two tufts of tawny hair sprout like small oases in the middle of the powerful desert of his shoulders. He wanted to take the wheel of our Topolino in order to try it out, but the poor "compact" sagged on its left wheel and refused to move.

The Abruzzese abhors the small. He says that from the *sfetature* of the hen, meaning the eggs as small as pigeon eggs, the basilisk serpent is born, that is to say the devil. Basilisk is also what he calls the undersized fetus produced by a woman, who in this case has not given birth to a child, but *ha fatte 'nu bascialische.* A legend cited by Athenaeus gives the origin of this superstition and the explanation of the word "basilisk." A king of the Spartans had taken as his wife a woman of short stature, while his subjects complained that in this way they were planning not to produce a king but a kinglet: *non rex sed regulus,* and in Greek *basiliscos.*

At the edge of the Pineta di Pescara is a sign: "Pineta Dannunziana." I am not blinded by love for the poetry of d'Annunzio. I pride myself on being one of the very few Italians completely immune to d'Annunzianism. Besides I was absent from Italy at the time of the great d'Annunzian fervor, and it may be for this reason that things concerning d'Annunzio now strike me as so new. I gaze with curiosity on the little forest, which I know to have been his "inspiration." It upholds with elegance the tall trunks of its pine trees, ostriches of the vegetable kingdom. In response to my wonder, the pine grove frees itself from its arboreal nature and takes on the shape of a woman. Thus is anthropomorphism born.

Sadness, the great burden of giants, is lacking in Concezio. Grave affliction darkens the brow of the Farnese Hercules, and bends his body over his cudgel. "The sculptor," writes Schlegel, "has depicted the son of Alcmene after one of his famous labors." As though before the labor the son of Alcmene had been a jolly fellow.

The rule conceals the truth, and the exceptions are so many "whys" scattered here and there like marking stakes. Concezio is an exception, an amiable monster, a kobold's soul in the body of Gyges. *Mens agitat molem.*

The house where we are staying was not always used for habitation. Concezio's grandfather took part in the parliamentary life of the first legislatures, and had given this house a political function. During the electoral campaign he would gather the sixty or seventy voters who constituted the majority in the municipality and keep them shut up in this house until election day, wining and dining them unstintingly. "My grandfather," concludes Concezio, "was never defeated." And how could he have been, if he treated those lucky prisoners to the same wine that today glistens on the table in our honor, and has been pressed from these vines that run in ordered, verdant rows down the slope on which our host's little house stands and climb the slope of the opposite hill across the valley? It is the whitest wine imaginable, the albino of wines, and terribly deceptive. The glass, when full, looks empty; but what soul in this wine transparent as the breath of a newborn baby, what fire! Johannisberg or Chablis do not stand up by comparison.

While we drink to Bacchus Lyaeus (Bacchus who loosens: so much truth in this word!), the parent bunches hang plump from the pergola over our heads, swept by fumes and illusions.

A curious village! Heavy and very light at the same time, northern and at the same time Greek. Around it a solidified tempest of mountains and valleys. At the top of each "wave" sits a little village with the hump of its large church and the upraised finger of its bell tower. These little villages have been built stone by stone by dark, patient little men who gradually emerged from the valleys, but their lofty position, their nestlike appearance suggest rather that they were built from above by those bird men whom Cyrano de Bergerac met on his extraordinary travels. Cyrano was a light poet, with an unraveled imagination, and how different, how much better than the verbose clown that Rostand filled with hot air and alexandrines and a few old windbags still tote around on our stages like a model of poetry. Rostand was of that dangerous species that spoils everything it touches. Cyrano's tirades have echoed in our military life, from the latrines in the barracks. What fascination does this poetry have for the soldier at the moment of relieving himself?

One of the little villages that can be seen from our host's pergola is called Turi. A great melancholy used to descend from time to time on the Turians. One by one they would go outside the village, scatter themselves among the vineyards or in the shadows of the olive trees, aim their double-barreled shotguns under their chins, and blow off their heads like corks from a bottle of spumante. All the men in these parts are hunters.

Another of these rocky little villages, which you can see from the road leading to Francavilla, is Miglìanico. Its church is even larger and more humped than the others, and its bell tower more "didactic." It was in the church of Miglìanico that Francesco Paolo Michetti saw the scene that inspired him to paint *Il voto* (The Vow). The figures in this famous painting are posed in creeping motions; the peasant in the foreground, prone on the floor of the church and resting on the tips of his fingers, is executing one of the better known Müller gymnastic exercises. These figures are not performing an act of devotion as one might have thought, but practicing a ritualistic rubbing cure. Phenomena of religious mass psychosis are quite frequent in these parts, but Michetti himself may not have been aware of the real reason for these positions. In Sulmona, up until a few years ago, those afflicted with stomachache used to go and sit on *Saint Pamphilus' chair.* Those suffering from rheumatism go and rub the ailing part on the walls of the church. More curious is the fact that in Ari (the village where we find ourselves) those with lumbago go and rub their backs not on the holy walls of the church, but on the wall of the town hall, or else on a rural boundary stone. Simultaneously they repeat three times:

> *Tèrmene, che sti piandäte,*
> *Famm'aresajje' 'sti lumme che mme se n'è ccaläte.*

> (Stone, well planted in the earth,
> Lift up these fallen loins of mine.)

We have taken the information on these rubbing rituals from *Miti, leggende e superstizioni dell'Abruzzo* by Giovanni Pansa (vol. I, chap. 5), and by a happy coincidence it is the very granddaughter of this illustrious scholar from Sulmona who is giving us such gracious hospitality in her pleasant country house.

There are valid reasons to support the idea of the bird origins of these rocky little villages. Bird men abound in these parts, and a very common surname in Abruzzo is Celidonio, which surely comes from *chelidon,* swallow.

What a pity! The cutting flight of this bird of spring (in spring itself there is something disagreeable), its shrill and vexing cry, are disturbing and a reminder that madness lies waiting. *Est in arundinis modulatio musica ripis.* The myth of the three swallow sisters is significant. Athena had entrusted to Aglauros, Herse, and Pandrosos a basket in which she had hidden Erichthonius, with the express command not to open it. But the three sisters could not resist their curiosity, whereupon they were set upon by the Furies and threw themselves over a cliff, being transformed at that same instant into swallows. Beware of the swallow! If she could speak, the "little nun" would invite us to suicide. And to think that the swallow passes for a "bearer of good tidings," while the poor bat, which if nothing else is a mammal like you and me and sucks its mother's milk, is so despised and feared!

At dinner, the day before yesterday, the courses followed each other as numerous and copious as ever, but without meat. Then I remembered it was Friday. In Abruzzo, prime considerations are more alive than elsewhere, the stony gaze more felt of those Mothers whom Faust descended into the bowels of the earth to interrogate. What power has the mountain over man's religious mind? These mountain walls transform the village into a natural temple, and geography has placed the man of Abruzzo in the favored place of prayer and faith. Here the expectation of a miracle is a living hope, as is for us the expectation of love, happiness, or fame. Abruzzo is a vast crèche that moves to the sound of bagpipes.

Ari, 14 August

Yesterday morning, Sunday, while driving down to Francavilla, we met an old woman who was walking along the dusty road, wearing, like a black monument, the heavy accumulation of her holiday clothes. It was Assunta, a peasant who works for our hosts. Every Sunday at dawn she sets out from Ari and walks the thirty kilometers separating it from Pescara, in order to pay her respects to her son, an apprentice in a machine shop. She takes him two eggs and a little fresh cheese; then slowly she returns, dragging her tower of dark clothes in the dust, and in the middle of the night she is back in Ari.

Instead of praising this maternal devotion, I ask why the mother goes down to visit the son rather than the son going up to visit the mother.

The past is eager for adventures, but without reciprocity. That young apprentice probably feels that by returning from the city to the village, he would betray that destiny which, like the locomotive, has eyes only for looking in front of itself. Legend (Lot's wife) joins with philosophy (Weininger) in exhorting man not to turn around.

We stop at a spring to drink. Women and children are standing around in Anacreontic poses, basins resting on one hip. Every spring is a dispenser of life: this one moreover dispenses miracles. But it doesn't show it, and even those who are miraculously cured remain in ignorance. We are told that neither Fiuggi water, nor Tettuccio, nor Chianciano can equal the virtues of this water, which flows freely and generously for everybody. But why waste a diuretic and cathartic water to wash salad and rinse clothes? The owner of this spring has been converted to Buddhism and spends many hours of the day kneeling before a blank wall, as though before an invisible altar. The race of Schopenhauers is not yet extinct, and Buddha teaches one to be lavish with good. We too took a long drink from the miraculous spring, but with no effect. Are we therefore unreceptive to miracles?

Guardiagrele, 15 August

We left early for Guardiagrele. The name of this city has a military ring to it. D'Annunzio calls it "city of stone," which is like saying nothing. Unless you're referring to Russian cities prior to the reign of Ivan III, the word "city" naturally evokes the idea of stone. The historian of Guardiagrele lived in the sixth century, but his name was like that of any of us: Pasquale Carlini. Pasquale Carlini's manuscript was preserved by the Benedictines of San Clemente a Comino. "Grele," says Pasquale Carlini, "was situated on what was almost a plain, east of the Majella. It was destroyed by a severe earthquake in the year A.D. 83. It had existed for 1200 years before the Christian era and was named for a temple that stood on the site where today stands the church of the Virgin Mary, a temple dedicated to the Sun, that is, to Apollo, also called Helios. Temples built to Jove, Janus, and Diana remain and are used today for Christian worship. The Samnites called it Aelion, the Greeks Graelio, from the name of their leader, the Romans Grelium, whence Greli, and the barbarians Graele, Graelle, Grela, and later Guardia di Graelle, Guardiagrele."

No greater suffering . . . You must travel by these secondary roads, where even today your vehicle is followed by a twisting plume of dust like the tail of a comet, to understand the great virtue of paved roads.

We go through Filetto and Orsogna. Despite its name, we do not find in Filetto so much as a *filetto di benzina,* a trickle of gasoline, and not even a pharmacy retailing this precious liquid. What do the inhabitants of Filetto use for spot-remover?

The name of Orsogna sounds as though it were invented by Gabriele d'Annunzio. They say that when the news reached Orsogna of its first soldier killed in war, the voice not only of his mother but of all the mothers of Orsogna was raised in the night and crackled until dawn, like the flame of a vast conflagration. The natural scenery of tragedy that surrounds this village also rouses the characters of tragedy, and their voices. Aeschylus is more Abruzzese than Eleusian.

Guardiagrele appears to the motorist like New York to the navigator. This reduction does not bother anyone who knows how to look at things with Greek eyes, that is, to see the large in the small. In order to paint his dragons, Böcklin took as his model those little fish that we eat head, tail, and all, and which are called smelts. This "insular" city is girdled with skyscrapers. Minuscule skyscrapers, of two or three stories at the most, but skyscrapers all the same for the proportion between width and height. Let me add that the skyscrapers of Guardiagrele are not the product of rhetoric and ambition, like those of San Babila in Milan or Piazza Castello in Turin, but of specific reasons of space. Like that of

Manhattan, the area of Guardiagrele is also enclosed within strict limits.

At this point our journey becomes sonorous. The sight of the skyscrapers awakens a vein of melody in Concezio. The automobile is filled with a Guardiagrele song, a mountaineers' tune. Concezio and the two *citeli* sing the melody, and the Signora Mariangela does the counterpoint. In Abruzzo children are called *citeli* or *quadrali.* The song is as solemn and melancholy as befits an Abruzzese song, but how can you follow its languid inflections when Concezio starts driving with his left hand and beating time with his right, while the automobile careens fearfully on the brink of ravines and precipices?

Cement is the "vulgarity" of our time. Alongside the most ordinary stone, the block of cement is like a wax nose stuck on a face of flesh. In addition to soul, cement lacks inwardness. It is as empty and dismal as a dead thing. Compare the ignobleness of damaged cement with the touching nobility of damaged marble. It is hard to understand why in a quarry of beautiful and living stones such as Italy they should build with cement, but there is a reason, and it is not facility but a certain kind of art. The *ideal* of the bad sculptor is to represent, by means of the materials of which statuary makes use, that which by its nature is quite different from the hardness and inflexibility of these materials, i.e., the soft, the supple, the delicate. Compare this "ideal" with the "ideal" of the bad poet to *express the inexpressible.* Bernini cut marble as though it were Provolone cheese, but Art Nouveau found in cement the way to surpass even

Cavalier Bernini, and the aspiration to give full flight to draperies, full quiver to foliage, and full swell to waves was achieved.

The public gardens of Guardiagrele have duly been called "the balcony of Abruzzo," because they overlook, if not really all, a great many of the Abruzzese mountains and valleys. Near the terrace slumbers an artificial pond, spanned by a cement bridge. The balustrade of the bridge is of cement and imitates interwoven tree trunks.

Under the garden trees, our gaze meets the nocturnal gaze, laden with unfulfillable dreams, of a dark-haired young woman. She is sprawled rather than seated on a bench, next to an elderly gentleman, with straw hat and pince-nez, who is quietly reading a newspaper. And we had thought that Emma Bovary was dead . . .

There is also an artificial pond in the public gardens of Ortona, and the cement bridge spanning it also has a balustrade made in imitation of interwoven tree trunks. Ortona is a splendid little city and its high promenade above the sea is worthy of a wounded and sorrowing Tristan. But also in Ortona there is the monument to Francesco Paolo Tosti. The "Master of Melody" (I transcribe the inscription on the monument) is shown bearded and with bags under his eyes in the form of a squeezed and very narrow bust, above a troop of maidens in nightgowns who sing and hold hands. I recommend as a detail of the modeling the folds of the nightgowns. Onatas the sculptor, before setting his hand to his famous statue of Hera, summoned the goddess to visit him in a dream and instruct him how she wanted to be portrayed. The composer of "Torna caro ideal" also visited his sculptor in a dream, but arrived too late. Judging by the confidences once made to me by a dead man during a spiritualist seance, the weakness and impotence of the dead is of the utmost. So how could a dead man prevent a crime?

A crazier wind has blown over the public gardens of Guardiagrele, at the point where gardens and town meet. There stands a building, or rather the "ghost" of a building, similar in kind to that "medieval village" that since the time of the 1911 Universal Exposition in Turin has been mirrored in the waters of the Po.

We are told that the columns and low vaults of this structure are built by the Pater method, which, like the nests of swallows, is a mixture of straw and cement. Why think of the abbey of Mont Saint-Michel and other distant and costly antiquities? Although it is the youngest ruin I know (it goes back to 1931 and was intended as a hotel, but the enterprise failed before construction was completed), this fake ruin can give, with a little mental effort, the same impressions given by any true one, and which are always the same: struggles between men and worship of God. Between this edifice produced by the imagination of Bouvard and Pécuchet and the Madame Bovary on the park bench, we find the best of Flaubert's work summed up in the public gardens of Guardiagrele.

So as to come into contact once again with natural things, we enter the workshop of Pasquale De Luca and Son, makers of oxcarts. Pasquale De Luca (is it the father or the son?) wears steel-rimmed spectacles and his shoulders are stooped from toil. The workshop of this shabby demiurge is full of wheels, hubs, and spokes. In the rear a "tilted" window looks out on an endless jumble of hills combed and coiffed like the background of a "primitive" painting. On one side are the crude pieces, on the other the finished and painted ones. A lady who is with us remarks that she prefers the unfinished pieces. We ask her why. "Because what is bare we can fill with our souls . . ." This is how the Noras are born, who at the end of the third act abandon the home that their souls have been unable to fill. A great misunderstanding underlies this search for simplicity. Like Eleonora Duse one performs without gestures, or takes Greek statuary as a standard, especially if one doesn't know that Greek statues were painted from head to toe like crèche figurines.

One cart stands ready in the middle of the shop. It is painted all over, as shining and dazzling as the little chapel of Nicholas V in the Vatican. Tiny red flowers and green leaves are entwined around the yellow ring of the wheels. Multicolored threads encircle each hub as on the bulge of a top. On the sides, extraordinary flowers spurt from vases, and like spurts of water they arch and fall. A little angel, all head and wings, looks at you without seeing you; he smiles and yet is sad . . .

The cart is ready. All that remains is to harness the ox to the red shaft, attach the ring to his damp nostrils, bundle our *citeli* inside, and depart, O Maria, for the fields.

One evening, at the time of the political battles, a youth, wounded in a brawl, came to die in the workshop of Pasquale De Luca and Son. Traveling through the

Abruzzese countryside, we often meet an oxcart, full of *quadrali* and resounding with song. And each time, we again see a pale youth lying amid the spokes and hubs, a star of blood on his forehead and his eye dimming on this earth as many-breasted as Diana of Ephesus, on this sky navigated by a fleet of white clouds.

O Maria, listen to your Ixion: better for us a cart of these clouds than an oxcart.

And not to stop again.

Guardiagrele, 15 August

The church of Santa Maria Maggiore is built over an ancient temple of Apollo. Here the gentle mother of Christ coexists with the most foppish of the pagan gods. The Apollo Belvedere already has the "Hollywood disease." The facade of Santa Maria Maggiore is still too narrow; it does not yet have the full physiognomy of the churches of Abruzzo. This we find in Santa Maria della Tomba in Sulmona, and especially in the splendid church of Collemaggio in L'Aquila. Not only is the architectonic structure admirable on the facade of this church, but also that infinite variety of pink that carries us so far away from the tonal experiments of Cézanne. The facades of the churches of Abruzzo are broad and bare. The portal creates a little temple with its diminishing columns and pointed top; a large rose window marks the center of the upper floor. This and nothing else. We will call it a "facade of sincerity." Seen in human terms, the church facades of Abruzzo express astonishment. Some have seen in Bernini's colonnade the arms of the Catholic Church open to receive the flock. We find a warmer, less materialized, more metaphysical reception in the church facades of Abruzzo. Very wide in comparison to the tiny mouth, they remind us of certain friendly faces: particularly that of Mario Broglio, painter and publisher of *Valori Plastici,* the magazine that played such an important role in the formation of the new Italian art. They also remind one of the astonished look of the skate fish.

In the churches of Abruzzo there is less rhetoric but more song than in many other very renowned and famous churches. Saint Peter's is a result of circumstance and, for all its difference in quality, a sort of anticipation of the Victor Emmanuel Monument.

Between the churches of Abruzzo, joined by their older sisters in Apulia, and across so many lands and the barrier of the Alps, flows a duet with the churches of the North, Cologne Cathedral, the Black Virgin of Chartres. Churches, too, manifest that mysterious affinity that from North to South unites souls, customs, and moods. Dostoevsky is reborn in Sicily. Secret veins wind underground, over the longest spaces. In the Algerian department of Constantine, I was shown a marble quarry that the natives claimed was the other end of the marble of Carrara, crossing beneath the sea and coming out again down there. But this may be only an idle boast.

It is eleven o'clock. We enter the cathedral of Guardiagrele. It is dedicated to the Virgin, and since today is 15 August, Feast of the Assumption, the service is particularly solemn. The walls between one chapel and another are draped in red. One approaches the church by a short flight of steps, between a double balustrade of marble. The cathedral is divided into two superimposed levels, like the last act of *Aida*. The new church was built above the primitive church, and that one, as I said, was originally a temple of Apollo. The new church is rectangular, lacking apses and the side hollows of chapels. The roof is flat, the decoration rich but second-rate. As we enter, the voices of the choral mass resound, and the chords on the organ pass like gusts of wind. The children's voices ring clear, even the red decorations on the walls sing, the color transformed into sound; but the dull sonority of the organ fills the spaces and muffles by its fullness.

Black and pyramidal, the women kneeling on the pavement appear as an assembly of giant penguins. These palmipeds are by now the only creatures that maintain faith in and respect for parliamentary traditions. An accommodating guide shows us on the right-hand wall the most important picture in the church: a painting doubly enclosed within a wooden frame and a mat of arabesqued cloth. It is a strangely modernistic painting, a more patient and childish Raoul Dufy. Caravels are seen poised like doves above a Gulf of Naples viewed as in a dream, their white sails billowing against the background of a flaming and smoking Vesuvius. Facing it, a less suggestive painting shows the Blessed Giovanni De Luca, from Guardiagrele, praying to the Virgin for the victory of Don John of Austria at the battle of Lepanto.

We yearn for the secret of men and things. We loathe those who, before letting us into their homes, run to close all the doors as though to hide the *corpus delicti*, and then welcome us with affected smiles and surround us with formalities in an anonymous little sitting room that has nothing to do with their own real life and that of their families.

Our accommodating guide does not belong to this odious species; he takes us into the sacristy of Santa Maria Maggiore and puts us in contact with the secrets of the temple. How to hide our emotion? This offering of trust is a confession of love. Here we do not find the concentration of the holy service, the august silence, the solemn voice of the officiant. We are backstage in the church. Priests and altar boys circulate hurriedly and speak aloud. The sacristy is white and filled with light. Like all the windows in Guardiagrele, the window of the sacristy of Santa Maria Maggiore also looks out on a boundless and magnificent panorama. Benches are stacked in a corner, some church trappings, two wooden candelabra painted with purpurin. On the floor lie withered flowers taken from the altars. Flowers are either sad or impudent: these are sad. We approach a half-open door and notice the organist seated at the keyboard of the organ behind the main altar. He is a young man with a small black mustache. Certain that no one can see him, he has the relaxed attitude of women when they know that no man is watching them. He is seated "comfortably" and a bit slumped; he loosens his collar with his free hand, and scratches his thigh, pinching the skin under the cloth of his trousers. He improvises modulations, sings in a tenor voice, and in the intervals yawns like a young leopard. As we tiptoe away, the admonishing voice of the preacher arrives from the church.

We go down a rustic stairway into a room corresponding to the sacristy and probably reserved for meetings of the clergy. Before a small table that functions as a pulpit are arranged several rows of those black metal armchairs upholstered in red velvet and welded together that used to be found in movie theaters. Before leaving the sacristy, the accommodating guide insisted on showing us the "treasure" of Santa Maria Maggiore; he took the cross carved by Nicola da Guardiagrele from a cupboard and made it revolve on its base so that we could admire it from all sides. It is a splendid example of the goldsmith's art, with a wealth of human figures and finely carved ornaments.

From the clerical meeting room we pass into the lower church. This is the ancient and most beautiful part. The lower church is more "mystical" than the upper one. Squat columns and low vaults support the ceiling. Rather than inviting you, ancient churches "force" you to pray. At the back, opposite the main altar, there are still the sacrificial altars of the pagan temple, transformed into Christian altars.

Conspicuous above the main altar is a statue of Saint Roch, enclosed in a glass case and skillfully placed against a window that surrounds it with light. It is a "trick," similar to Bernini's "glory" in Saint Peter's, but more rustic and naive. The statue of the saint is of wood, painted like the figureheads on the prows of sailing ships. Saint Roch delicately lifts the left hem of his tunic, exposing on his thigh a small red spot similar to the mouth of a newborn baby. It is a therapeutic gesture: Saint Roch is the healer of tumors. A dog seated at his feet raises his head and looks at his master with eyes warm with loyalty.

As we go back along the Via Roma, the mild giant who acts as our mentor stops to say hello to a lady seated at the door of her house. We find this custom pleasing because it replaces the café and brings the drawing room into the middle of the street. Why shouldn't it be practiced in large cities as well? It would be good to see conversation gradually take the place of traffic, and mechanical civilization yield to the civilization of manners.

Literature too has its rhabdomancers: the lady whom Concezio stopped to greet is the sister of the poet Modesto Della Porta, who died some years ago of a malignant tumor. The healing virtue of Saint Roch does not always achieve the desired effect. Donna Concetta dresses in black and her eyes bear the red rings that signify a marriage to grief.

The archive of the muses will record two Modests: Modest Mussorgsky and Modesto Della Porta, the second more modest than the first. Della Porta was a poet and tailor, just as Hans Sachs was a poet and shoemaker. While Donna Concetta leads the way up the steep little flight of stairs, our mentor confides to us that the white linen suit he is wearing was made for him by "poor Modesto" shortly before his death.

Modesto Della Porta's muse stood somewhere between the sentimental and the sarcastic. Modesto collected the themes for his poetry from the living voices of craftsmen, with whom he liked to stop and converse. His house is surrounded by blacksmiths, carpenters, shoemakers, working in the middle of a continual click-clack. His morality (dialect poets are more moralizing than those employing the standard language) is neither uplifting nor catastrophic, but modest like his name.

The people are teleological. The questions "What does it mean?" and "What's it for?" are essentially their kind of questions. Mental growth leads to a progressive renunciation of the purposes of our works and their presumed rewards. Which does not happen through indifference, nor lack of interest, nor "materialism," but through an acquired awareness of the present, and the possibility of considering the "metaphysical" background of things, their immutable and eternal essence. The people "have no present" and therefore no joy. The people are a river flowing slowly in the direction of a fabulous country, where all the reasons are gathered, all the purposes, all the "whys," all the rewards for the things we gradually do or must do, by our will or the will of others. Motionless on the banks, the metaphysical man watches the river flow by, and a great melancholy shrouds his gaze, since he knows that that fabulous land does not exist. Poems, the things he does by art, his games, do not correspond to any "why." And the people as they pass look at him, and do not understand why he goes on doing these things — playing these "games."

Abruzzo loves this poet and Guardiagrele worships him. Whenever two people stop to talk, Modesto's bitter and sarcastic verses enter to form part of the conversation. We were present at one such encounter. We were embarrassed and bored stiff. There ought to be a footnote in the etiquette manuals instructing people not to speak in the presence of third parties of things of which those third parties are ignorant. Like all dialect poets,

Modesto Della Porta placed the "mother" theme before all others. Motherhood is the deep note of simple minds.

O Ma', se quacche notte mi ve' immente
ti vùjje fa' na bella 'mpruvisate;
t'àja minì a purtà na serenate
'nche stu trumbone d'accumpagnamente.

(O Ma, if some night I get the idea
I'd like to give you a nice surprise,
I'll come and sing you a serenade
accompanied by this trombone.)

Modesto Della Porta's poems have been collected in a volume by the publisher Carabba, under the title *Ta-pù*. We start leafing through *Ta-pù*. . . The geographer Paganel, who accompanied Lord Glenarvan in search of Captain Grant, studied Spanish during the voyage, but when he tried to speak it with the Patagonian Thalcave, he realized that what he had learned was Portuguese. Faced with the poems of Modesto Della Porta, we too realize that we have picked the wrong language.

Francesco De Sanctis writes: "The specific role of culture is to stimulate new ideas and less material needs, to form a more educated and civilized class of citizens, to put them in contact with foreign culture, and to bring languages closer and unite them, developing in them not what is local but what they have in common." And on the previous page, as though to give a warning example: "With the waning of culture, dialects prevail." We fully share the opinion of our worthy Minister of Education, and would only add that for us dialects are closed worlds, islands that may be beautiful, but on which we will never land.

Concetta Della Porta was for Modesto what Henriette Renan was for Ernest, Liesbeth Nietzsche for Friedrich, Paolina Leopardi for Giacomo. And now that Modesto is no more, Donna Concetta keeps watch over his memory. Everything in the drawing room has stayed "as it was when he was here": the bric-à-brac, the consoles, the little bamboo tables, the Josephine Baker doll sprawled on the sofa, the "Turkish" rugs, the postcards arranged fanwise on the wall, the photographs of Salvatore Di Giacomo, Angelo Musco in a straw hat, Francesco Paolo Michetti . . . We go up to the bedroom and out on the roof terrace, to see the wicker armchair in which poor Modesto, without realizing it, breathed his last.

The chair is green, placed a little sideways, and no one has sat in it since "that" day. Pieces of furniture collect the spirit of their owners and become characters in their own right. Left alone, the armchair continues to look out over the endless plain, and down there the outline of Chieti, above which rises, thin as a thread, the bell tower of the church. In his final days, Modesto said of himself that he was like fireworks on which it had rained beforehand.

We take another look at the armchair. It is in excellent condition. When it rains, they drag it inside, then when the weather clears they put it back on the terrace, a little sideways, in the consecrated position. Piety, too, has its stage settings.

Next to the poet's house is another house, and its windows are closed with shingled blinds. Their color is that beautiful Veronese green of the shutters of our adolescence, when the face of the beloved girl dawned amid the geraniums. Then we notice that these shutters are of iron, and the shingles overlap in the shape of pointed leaves, turned downward to let a little air pass through. Why such protective measures? Walking around the town, we find other similarly armored blinds. Lying at the foot of the Majella, this severe city is "the mountain" by antonomasia. Its sentinel name evokes the idea of snow, of long shut-in winters. Even the songs of Guardiagrele recall, through the melancholy "decline" of autumn, the silent and pious absorption of winter:

Lu ciele è chiuse e chiuse è la montagne.
Le foje giale casche a une a une.
Sempre sa nebbie, amore, gna si coje
La live e casche a l'albere le foje.

(The sky is overcast and the mountain hidden.
The yellow leaves fall one by one.
Always this fog, my love, the olives
Are picked and the leaves fall from the tree.)

In large cities we forget the "social" function of the church (I mean in the plastic sense, "for the eye," so to speak); we are therefore struck by this role of a hen with chicks played by the church in villages and small towns, or, in human terms, of a mother with her children. Here the expression "mother church" regains its literal significance. We look at the cathedral of Guardiagrele, its bare stone facade, its arched portal, its window, its rose window, its sturdy bell tower; we observe how maternally it crouches in the midst of its children, and how they circulate around it, walking or resting, speaking or keeping silent, and from it, from its age-old and watchful wisdom, drawing tranquillity in behavior, peace of mind, and faith in this life and in the next.

Along the right side of the cathedral runs a portico with columns, and under it glows what little remains of a colossal saint painted in fresco. Motorists, say hello to Saint Christopher. The figure of the saint of Herculean stature who swam across the sea carrying the Redeemer on his shoulders has that look of being "seated in the void" that painters gave their subjects before the invention of verismo. It is the work of Andrea da Lecce. The leading painter of Guardiagrele had a terrible name: he was called Delitto [Crime].

Farther along, under the same portico, the coats-of-arms of the barons of Guardiagrele are arrayed like seals of stone. We read the names of the De Sorte family, the Vallereggia, the Scioli, the Comino, the Ugni. In the shadows of these strong men, saints or barons (baron comes from *barüs*, meaning "strong" and "heavy"), flourish the small local trades: ironware and cordage at the feet of Saint Christopher, tomatoes under the barons' shields.

As we take these notes, people stop and stare at us, come to their windows, and to the doorways of their shops. Is there anything wrong with taking notes? A short and obviously hunchbacked man tags along with us for a while and never takes his eyes off us. He is visibly anxious to know the purpose of our investigation. It increasingly dawns on us that this rummaging in the lives of others, this unearthing of secrets, is one of the most insane forms of curiosity.

But they are not secrets of the soul: they are secrets of the city. What difference does that make? Cities, just like the most secretive souls, have their shames, their jealously guarded lives, which ought not to be disturbed, much less uncovered. The Italian people's repugnance for certain extreme forms of psychologism probably comes from this "tact" that needs to be preserved before the secrets of others, this respect for the "closed door." So shall we give up our "urban Ibsenism"? No, but from now on we will withdraw to one side in order to jot down our discoveries.

The prow of Guardiagrele is turned resolutely toward the Majella and lifts in the wind, like the stump of a broken antenna, the ruined tower next to which they used to shoot brigands. People from around here call this place *lu piano,* the upper level.

The years will never extinguish in the man the mind of the boy to the point where the word "brigand" cannot still kindle a blaze in us. Our curiosity expands like a epidemic, infects the people around us, and climbs up to the terrace of a nearby house. There are two old women there, one of them very old indeed. "Grandmother," says the one less old, "knew those times... Grandma, tell what you know." The grandmother begins to speak as in a dream, but how is one to grasp that trembling murmur from down here, extract its particles of words, line them up, and interpret them? After a long wait loaded with silence, the old woman appears at the doorway of the house, surrounded by family members who hold her upright like a wooden idol.

Her head is almost bald, and covered with brown spots. When the old woman opens her mouth, all that appears is a black hole. What little remains to her of her eyes is encircled by blood, two poor "wounds" inside the huge, dark disks of the eyesockets. From under her nose, where it meets the mouth, hang the long and spiny hairs of her mustache. At the time of the brigands she was six years old. Someone nearby adds, "And now she's ninety-five." Does she still remember *lu briganti*? Yes, and one in particular named Domenico Di Sciascio. He was not a brigand by vocation, but secret ties bound him to the government of Franceschiello, the last Bourbon king of Naples, and when Abruzzo passed under the crown of Savoy, Domenico Di Sciascio and his two brothers took to the hills. A born leader, Domenico recruited two hundred men as his followers. He had an agreeable nature. He used to tie a false beard under his chin and go and sit in the cafés of Guardiagrele. Everybody recognized him, but no one bothered him. He was crazy about opera. In the winter he used to go to Rome, and wearing his false beard enjoyed the performance from a seat in the Argentina theater.

They put a price on Domenico Di Sciascio's head, and one day while he was taking a siesta, a member of his gang fired a pistol in his ear and wounded him. It was Saturday, the only day in the week when Di Sciascio ran the risk of getting wounded. Di Sciascio was devoted to the Madonna, and on Saturday, the day consecrated to the Madonna, he went around unarmed. They picked him up and carried him to the place of execution, but in the face of death, Domenico pulled himself together and stood up.

At this point the old woman's memories come back to life more vividly. From the ashy circles of her eye-sockets, the poor bloodshot eyes flash sparks. "What a handsome man!" She clasps on her breast the two withered plane-tree leaves that have taken the place of her hands. "He was wearing slate-gray trousers with a red stripe on the side, and a red polka-dot shirt." And the same interlocutor as before: "To anticipate the gunshot wounds. . . ."

One of the "types" enumerated by Lombroso is the "bandit's woman," blindly devoted to the strong and criminal man, and the more she is mistreated, the more she is beaten, the more she loves him. Would this near centenarian perhaps be one of them?

The old woman continues: "The drums rolled, fathers boxed their children's ears so that they'd see what happens to those who don't submit to authority, and everyone, men, women, and children, cried their hearts out."

We ask the old woman, "Why did they cry?" And she, in a voice that trembles not from age but from recovered emotion:

"Because he was *no simile,* a fellow creature."

It is the most "Christian" utterance we have heard for some time in these parts.

When the informer went to collect the reward, not

only did they not give it to him, but they shot him too.
And the old woman laughs joyfully, exposing her black mouth.

TMP

TMP

THE MARLBORO PRESS

P.O. BOX 157

MARLBORO, VERMONT 05344

Francavilla, 16 August

For Protagoras the sophist the circle stood for perfection. We prefer the angle, the rectangle, the square. Those who praise Giotto for his O do not know the injury they are doing him. If Cubism had no other quality, we would still love it solely for its poetry of angles. Who will extol the stupidity of the curve? We appreciate the hygienic reasons that have caused the corners to be rounded in modern houses, but the metaphysics of the room thereby *suffer.* The circle is also the sign of immortality. We do not care for that inhuman condition, we do not wish for it, and confidently await an all-too-human death.

Francesco Paolo Michetti loved circular forms. There was something of the mystagogue about him. Is it to imitate the form of the eye that the windows of his studio in Francavilla are round? (For us, the poetry of the window is still enclosed within the precise rectangle.) They look like two enormous eyes, one staring at the sea, the other at the pine grove.

They tell us that Michetti built this studio himself, about sixty years ago. A singular construction! Between

Gothic and Art Nouveau. Bare bricks reveal the texture of the wall externally. Narrow vertical glass windows cleave the entire height of the building. Bull's-eye windows complete its connections with the outside. On the seaside facade, roots of arches emerge from the wall, seem about to thrust themselves up and curve inward, but stop just at the beginning of the thrust and, as though repenting, remain cropped. One is surprised to find clear, neat rooms inside such an astrological building. Two very large paintings occupy the studio: *Gli Storpi* (The Cripples) and *Le Serpi* (The Serpents). Painters used to take the greatest pains in priming their canvases, they sought with infinite patience to make their colors lasting, and wanted the painting to be, aside from what it represented, something admirable in itself, solid and brilliant as a jewel. Instead the weave of the canvas can be seen under the light coat of white lead that Michetti rapidly applied to the painting surface; and he went over this preparation, so inadequate to support and protect the painting, with a very thin tempera, similar to the kind used by stage designers. As a result of this scarcely resistant preparation, *Gli Storpi* and *Le Serpi* are flaking away and being reduced to dust. Michetti also made the frames himself, and these for *Gli Storpi* and *Le Serpi* are grooved and gilded, and decorated with twigs, berries, and shoots of grain. We look at a portrait of Signora Franca Florio, or rather of that portion of Signora Franca Florio extending from neck to mid-thigh, and on which that famous pearl necklace, so much talked about in the modest and peaceful Italy of 1905, shines with its moonlight beads. We search in vain for the psychological reason that induced Michetti, as in *La Figlia di Jorio,* to decapitate his figures. And yet Michetti too had his microcosm, which he tried to assemble in a number of small gouaches hastily brushed on random sheets of paper, sometimes on printed matter from the Senate. They are his last works. We linger over them sadly, as though to catch the last sounds of a dying voice.

We go up to the convent. Before it lies a grassy, rectangular, open space, on which rises a hillock bristling with pines and cypresses. The facade of the church, with the half-Moroccan bell tower rising above it, and the portico of the convent form the background. One of the arches frames the erect figure of the *Mastro* (as people from hereabouts still call Francesco Paolo Michetti) cast in bronze by the sculptor D'Antino. We have heard complaints that Michetti, "who had such an extraordinary gaze," is shown with his eyes closed, but unless the sculptor wanted to signify in that vacant stare the gaze par excellence of the spirit, the closed eyes could be a witty expedient to avoid statuary's natural aversion to imitating the gaze. To the right of the entrance, some letters of a mysterious language are traced on the wall. We are told that Michetti invented this language for his personal use. Why? Prison inmates use a secret language among themselves so as not to be understood by their jailers. Obviously, Michetti considered all humanity to be composed of jailers. Strange, this mania for concealment, in one who had so little to hide. There was a rural madness in Michetti, along with a form of prolonged adolescence. To show how difficult it is to read this introductory epigraph, we are told that *not even*

Gabriele d'Annunzio succeeded in interpreting it. The similarity to Apollonius of Tyana is obvious: this poet, too, was said to "know all languages." Abruzzo deifies its great men. Moreover, the omniscience of famous men is a dogma for the ignorant, who sometimes even make use of it as a weapon: "Who do you think you are — Dante Alighieri?" According to the most reliable version, the epigraph goes as follows: "Whoever brings evil into this house, may he be buried in dung." It is a legitimate wish and one that, for all we know, Providence has so far fulfilled. But why not express it in a clearer way? As for its appearance, Michetti's language looks like something between Sanskrit and Hebrew. Every mysterious language imitates Oriental characters. For simple minds, the East is the land of mysteries. Even Plato fell into this trap.

We are pleased. Finally we have found the living portrait of human dignity: Donna Annunziata Michetti comes toward us, her dress white, her hair white. In her, the model of the great Italian woman lives again. She is how we imagine the mothers of Rome, and the wives of its warriors and poets. Donna Annunziata also recalls Eleonora Duse, minus the intolerable cult of sorrow and the assumption therefore that life is only to be respected when it consists of suffering and resignation. And yet this "noble" lady was, we are told, a girl from the fields, which is actually how she appears in her splendid youth, in the "head" that occupies the center of the large wall of the studio, perhaps the best work painted by her "Cicillo."

Donna Annunziata accompanies us on our visit to the convent. Before becoming an artists' center, these walls sheltered the monastic life of the Franciscan friars, then of the Poor Clares. At the end of the corridor that skirts the little cloister is a round window, similar to those in the studio in the pines. We enter the workrooms. They look more like workshops and laboratories than painters' rooms or studios. A wind of alchemy blows between the white walls. Tables cluttered with test tubes, beakers, alembics, retorts, dark lanterns. A microscope stands ready to reveal the forms of microorganisms. Mechanical instruments are lined up on another table. On still another some three-color plates. "His" eyeglasses lie on the desk, along with "his" watch and ink bottles. Isolated to one side, the small globe on which Michetti followed the progressive "drying-up of civilization." "Civilization," Michetti said, "follows a slow but steady movement from the equator to the north pole, with no possibility of palingenesis or return, and leaves behind it silence and desolation." Michetti was completing Edouard Schuré. Michetti called this studio in which he loved to work and exercise his imagination his "brain-pan." In a corner, motionless and hidden by a white dust cover, "his" rocking chair. When the living have gone to bed and the convent is shrouded in silence, the lantern is lighted in the "brain pan" and the beloved ghost comes back to rock among his beakers and alembics. "Beware of thoughts that come in the armchair," Nietzsche warned, but he hadn't thought of rocking chairs. On a panel prepared for painting and leaning against the wall, a tiny bat clings by its feet and dangles like a little yellow sack. We assume it to be part of this necromancer's furnishings, but when Donna Annunziata pokes it with her finger, it reveals by the quickened throb of its minuscule thorax that it is living its diurnal night.

In the adjoining room are three towering white rollers, whose function we are unable to determine. A beret and a work smock hang on a diminutive clothes rack. What would they say if they could speak, these garments that mildly and patiently go on waiting for the hand of their master?

"Your master, O faithful companions, is still in your midst. He was more than a painter: he was one of those Leonardesque Italians, whose overflowing excess of wishes and ideas makes it impossible for them to concentrate on or perfect any one of them. Cosmic imaginations revolve inside the heads of these gentle demiurges. And so that their secrets do not fall into a world unworthy to receive them and incapable of understanding them, they consign them to a language known only to themselves."

The visit to the convent continues. Rooms and corridors are of a virginal whiteness. In the hall where the convent elders assembled for their meals, the credenza has been replaced by a small harmonium. A painting by Sartorio in his "early manner" hangs over a console. It is a Christian idyll. The figures already have that look of prognathous adolescents that he multiplied in his decorations for Parliament. The painter has signed with only his initials, without realizing that the initials for Giorgio Aristide Sartorio* spell the word "gas." Next door, we enter on tiptoe into the little cell where Gabriele d'An-

*Actually Giulio Aristide Sartorio. (Tr.)

nunzio wrote some of his most intense works. Hippolyte Taine's theory is flatly denied by this cell. Never again will we believe in the influence of the surroundings. For what good is so much neatness and this air of chastity if it was precisely in this cell that *L'Innocente* and *Il Piacere* were written? A mullioned window looks out on the orchard, and another, covered by a transparent curtain on which gleam some unreal flowers designed by Michetti and interwoven with sentences formulated in the usual mysterious language, looks toward the distant sea, while, immediately below, a group of athletic pine trees, like whimsical swimmers in the air, diagonally bend their muscular trunks before arriving at the crest of their foliage, then suddenly straighten out and with an arrogant shove of the elbow resume the direction of the sky. Donna Annunziata lifts her glass of vermouth and toasts: "To the health of Italy!"

At the time the convent was active, when in the cell known as "silentium" d'Annunzio was writing *Il Trionfo della Morte*, and in the old refectory of the Franciscan monks Michetti was painting *La Figlia di Jorio*, and on the little harmonium Francesco Paolo Tosti was composing "Vorrei morir quando tramonta il sol," and so on, whoever arrived first at the end of his labors ran to the courtyard of the church and started the bells ringing, to announce to the world that a new work of art was born. Simultaneously, in other parts of the world, other artists, very different from these, were in their turn finishing their own works, and albeit without ringing bells, were just as convinced of having given new riches to humanity. And these did not know of the others, nor the others of them. Likewise, in pagan authors of the first centuries you will seek in vain the names, the trace of those Christians who were arousing so much ardor for life and faith among their peoples. Who represented the truth and who was in error? The world is sufficiently vast, sufficiently "indifferent," to contain the illusions of both.

Pescara, 17 August

In front of d'Annunzio's house in Pescara, the spirit of poetry resides in arboreal symbols: an oak, an olive tree, a laurel rise out of the cement of the little piazza, closed off on one side by a wall, likewise of cement, with three empty niches. The middle niche holds a dry basin. Thc pomegranate is missing; it has been transplanted to the courtyard. Marietta, who was Donna Luisa d'Annunzio's maid and today is the custodian of the house, complains that the children of the quarter irreverently pluck the heraldic foliage. A human creature's destiny is sometimes hidden in his or her name: Marietta's name is Camerlengo [Chamberlain]. Certainly there is no lack of children in the quarter. The Via delle Caserme, which is a street of small craftsmen, passes in front of the d'Annunzio home. Standing before Athena's olive tree, we admire with all the envy, all the wonder inspired in us by the mystery of manual labor, a joiner who one by one inserts the teeth of a rake in the little holes in a planed piece of wood white as a fine slice of roast veal. Already one can smell the odor of grass and see the beauty of a garden. The name of the street that runs along the side of the house has been dictated by circumstance:

Via Gardone.*

One approaches the house through an atrium, enclosed by large glass windows with wrought-iron arabesques. The art of decorative restoration, which Luca Beltrami inaugurated many years ago in the Castello in Milan, has arrived down here. We cross the little courtyard with its well in the middle and green wooden lattices going up the stairs, on which creepers proliferate, and enter a gallery of low vaulted rooms. They are vast and deserted. The spell lasts for a few minutes, until logic succeeds in formulating the question: "What are we waiting for?" We are drawn by the void: it isolates our personality, and places us at the center of the universe. How ambitious is the search for solitude! Here is the stall, with a few logs and dry leaves heaped in a corner, where the boy Gabriele loved to hide. In the fascination we feel for the stall there is perhaps that same need for animal warmth that Nietzsche expressed in another way: "Give me warm hands, and warming hearts." And yet warm hands, not to mention sweaty hands, repel us. To arrive at fellow feeling, there is always a certain repulsion to be overcome. We go up to the gallery. In the first room a jacket is hanging on the back of a chair and a small turtle is diagonally crossing the brick floor. It is the genius of the place. No one knows when it was born. Donna Luisa found it in this house when she arrived as a bride. *Les dieux s'en vont, les tortues restent.* Another turtle crawls by itself in the

*From the site of d'Annunzio's villa, the Vittoriale, on the shores of Lake Garda. (Tr.)

gallery. It is much larger than the other but a child by comparison: it is only fifty years old and above all has no history.

We pause to look at, on the wall of the drawing room, *Tasso in the Sant'Anna Hospital, The Studio of Raphael,* and a nineteenth-century French print, *Rêverie,* so rosy and misty that we almost faint from languor. Some of our preferences are unmentionable. In the study of Don Francesco Paolo, a skull, crookedly covered by a floppy straw hat, leers from the top of a shelf. Behind a door we rediscover our childhood hanging on a nail: a big, rusty, and very light key. If you grasp it by the handle and hit it hard, you will see a crepe-paper star jump out of the tube. And if you're warm, you can use it as a fan. We cross the room in which the poet was born. Our gaze does not linger on the large brass bed. Wreaths with ribbons have been placed there. We enter the little room where Donna Luisa liked to spend her time. Here is the sewing machine, the armchair . . .

Why visit the houses of poets? Why rummage in their lives? Why disturb the gentle ghost of a mother?

We withdraw on tiptoe. Before going back out to the gallery, we meet the stare of a photograph. The bald skull, the pointed goatee, the slightly dimmed eye: there can be no mistake. Marietta, however, corrects us: it is Don Antonio, the poet's brother, who for many years has been living in "Broccolino," close to New York.

There is more than vain ambition in this "will to resemble." There is a touch of mysticism, a wish for communion, to receive a greater spirit into oneself, to deify oneself. I recall an individual in Florence who bore a natural resemblance to d'Annunzio, and had artfully perfected the precious likeness. Between five and six in the afternoon he would walk along the Via Tornabuoni with two greyhounds on a leash, and from the opposite shore of the Giacosa and Doney cafés the smart set greeted him with deference, themselves happy to pay their respects to the image of d'Annunzio, in the absence of the real one. The Cavalier Venceslao, a character in Gerolamo Rovetta's novel *L'Idolo,* tries to exploit the flattering ambiguity of his resemblance to Giuseppe Verdi. One day he is on a train standing in the Poretta station, and passengers on the train alongside think they recognize the maestro on his way to his annual cure at the Montecatini spa and improvise a sympathetic ovation. Venceslao appears at the train window and affably thanks them. In Tuscany resemblance overcomes death itself, or at least makes solitude less harsh. When the painter Ottone Rosai's father died, the son let his beard grow in order to resemble the deceased and perpetuate in this life the image of the man who had abandoned it. Then comes oblivion, a general resemblance.[1]

---

1. In Egypt, the passion for self-deification was manifested through disguise. Tutankhamen, in his tomb, was disguised as Osiris.

Sulmona, 18 August

We arrive in Sulmona at dusk. The Middle Ages had different names for this city, including *Salmona* and *Salamona*. I enjoy fortuitous meanings. A "bluestocking" city; a "salmon" city that ascends the icy current of rivers, turning the waters to silver . . .

The cathedral of Sulmona is also built on the ruins of a pagan temple. Originally this church was named for the Virgin, but at the beginning of the eighth century it took the name of Bishop Pamphilus, who is buried in it. Along with Ovid and Celestine V, this saint, "everyone's friend," completes the triad of Sulmona's tutelary genii. The facade of San Panfilo, a mixture of Gothic and Romanesque, is wide and wonderstruck in accordance with the style common to the splendid churches of Abruzzo.

Meanwhile the three tutelary genii contend for honors and priority. The insignia of Sulmona is composed of the four letters S.M.P.E., generally recognized as the four initials of the hemistich *Sulmo Mihi Patria Est.* But the canons of San Panfilo do not see it that way, and they read the four initials, repeated in the apse of the cathedral in fine Teutonic letters, as *Spes Mea Pamphilus Est*. Who is right? I once had an uncle and aunt. My uncle used to say, "Rome, city of the Caesars," to which my aunt would retort, "Rome, city of the popes." Nor did they realize that they were saying the same thing.

Concezio points his finger at the crouching shadow of Mount Morrone and says, "See that little light up there? That's the hermitage of Celestine V." When Celestine was elected pope, the people of Sulmona went up to the hermitage and bore him down triumphantly into the city. On Easter Monday, the faithful still gather in the nearby little church of Sant'Onofrio and celebrate. But for whom is that little light up there now burning? "There's a friar in Celestine's hermitage who came here from Cucullo," says Concezio, adding, "and before the friar there was an ex-soldier who set out to be a hermit, but he caught rheumatism and had to find himself a dryer refuge." These explanations do not convince us. Celestine liked to stay up late at night and converse with his friend Ovid.

Ovid and Celestine are the two major and conflicting genii of the Sulmona area: the second an agathodemon, a genius of saintliness and grace, the first a cacodemon, meaning an infernal spirit who finds no rest, molests wayfarers, and unleashes storms. And yet they understand each other. Celestine was fond of the soul of Ovid, just as Saint Gregory was fond of the soul of Trajan. He tried to pluck that soul from hell by celebrating many masses for it, but in vain. Anyway what would Ovid do in paradise? To paradise go albinos, vegetarians, and those who like the music of Don Lorenzo Perosi. They remained friends all the same and continued to talk to each other over the well of the monastery. As the people from hereabouts tell it: "While he was pope, Celestine studied the works of Ovid and ascertained that a large treasure was buried in the rubble of the poet's villa on the slopes of Mount Morrone. He decided to build the Abbey of the Holy Spirit in the vicinity of Sulmona, and had a beautiful plan drawn up. People looked at the plan and said, 'Holy Father, how will you be able to finish such a big building?' The pope replied, 'There may not be enough stones or mortar, but there's plenty of money.' No one knew that the pope was able to avail himself of a boundless treasure. Celestine resigned as pope, left Rome, and returned to the slopes of Mount Morrone, there where he had once done penance. Nights he would go and dig up the treasure, and he began transporting denarii to the place where he was planning to build the abbey. Construction started. Shovelfuls of money were needed but there was no lack of it. Every Saturday, when the workmen had to be paid, Celestine went to get three sacks of gold and three of silver. When the abbey was finished, the treasure closed up again. And no one since has been able to find out exactly where it is or how to go about finding it." Thus the abbey of Sulmona was built with the money of Ovid, necromancer and damned soul, just as many churches in Rome were built with columns and materials from pagan temples. Between Christianity and paganism there is strict collaboration.

The remains of Ovid's villa, which the natives here call the *potêche d'Uiddie,* crop out amid the wild vegetation below Celestine's hermitage. All that is left after twenty centuries is a massive wall with *opus reticulatum,* seventy meters long and from eight to nine meters high. The building had three stories. The second contained the gynaeceum, the galleries, the triclinia, the library; on the third were the recreation rooms, the museum, and the loggias. Beautiful gardens flourished on all sides; there was a laurel grove, indispensable to the home of a poet; and the air was filled with the vast twittering of the aviaries. As for the mortar that joined this huge building, it was the kind known as the "lime of seven powers," and it was called such because when Jesus Christ suffered his passion and death, a Pharisee threw in his face a handful of this lime, which from that moment lost its "seven powers" and became the kind of chalky stuff we still use today. Many mysteries of rational architecture can be explained in this way.

For a long time it was not understood why people around here used the word *potêche* for Ovid's villa, thus from the common meaning of *bottega* ascribing to the poet the activity of shopkeeper, in addition to those of saint, wizard, philosopher, and prophet. But *bottega* is a very old word, going back to the Greek *apothekai.* For the Romans it meant the *cellae ubi aliquid adservabatur,* i.e., the granary and storeroom, and in the Middle Ages it indicated the place where medicines were sold. Today we have *apothicaire,* pharmacist, in France, and in Germany *Apotheke,* pharmacy.

The *Fountain of Love* gushes forth beneath the ruins of the villa, and it is here that the poet had himself transported by litter late at night, sometimes to make love to a sorceress, sometimes to the emperor's daughter herself. The latter arrived from Rome by some very rapid means whose mechanism has unfortunately been lost, but the sorceress did not have to suffer from corns on her feet since she lived only a stone's throw away in the area of Santa Lucia. Basins, mosaics, and lead water pipes have been unearthed here. The pipes once went all the way to the top of Mount Morrone, and through them the shepherds of the Abbey of the Holy Spirit flooded the valley with milk. Under the administration of priests, life is continual enjoyment.

We start back toward the city. The shade in the Public Gardens is broken up by white shadows and brought to life by the evening promenade. The nubile girls of Sulmona go by in squads, abreast, holding each other's hands. Every obstacle yields to their proud march. A fresh breath flows across our faces, a mixture of natural odors and cheap perfume. Those who dream of *femmes fatales* and the embraces of vamps make me laugh. The secret of Venus lies in these simple hearts, these naive desires, these modest imaginings of love. How do these girls prepare their souls in the service of the goddess, how do they prepare their bodies? On Sunday morning they plunge their precious slimness in the kitchen tub and — O great mystery! — wash each portion of the gift for the man who will someday come.

Martial has said that for elegance and grace, the women of Sulmona rivaled those of Athens. For Pietro Paolo Parzanese, on the other hand, "the women around here have a *je ne sais quoi* of Gothic." As for Panfilo Serafini, he found that "the pretty girls of Sulmona transport you with their large dark eyes, and ensnare hearts with their long thick hair marvelously braided in a thousand ways." And us? We have no basis for judgment. We can tell you how the girls of Sulmona smell, not what they are made of: we have been close to them only once, and it was evening. Is it perhaps an advantage not to see but only to glimpse? Armando Spadini made a virtue of his nearsightedness and painted people and things as cloudy and vague. Beauty, moreover, is a creation of our eyes, our desires, our mood. "The Lord wanted the eye of Man to have this capacity, to let him believe that not all of the Earthly Paradise had been lost to him." And had we tried to embrace the women who one evening, at the end of summer, seemed to us so beautiful, they would have vanished like shadows, and our arms would have returned to our chest empty.

Sulmona's appearance is one of vigilant awareness. *Noblesse oblige.* Invisible but present, someone in this city is watching and judging. This arcane presence keeps life from becoming play, meanness, frivolity. One ought to walk on tiptoe, speak low, and keep one's mind on a grave and decorous level. The air all around is holy. We are proud that the Spirit that holds this land in thrall is the spirit of a Poet.

Even before entering the city, we became aware of the ineffable Presence in the countryside, over which the night lovingly stooped. We became aware of it below that strange village that straggles down from the mountain, vainly held at the top by the ruins of its castle, and which we were told is called Pacentro. Shortly thereafter, continuing along Highway 17, we found the crossroads and the road to the left that leads to the Celestine abbey, now converted into a prison. The huge ghost gravely circulates in these parts, and its sadness, which all these centuries have been unable to mitigate, fills the earth and sky.

Sulmona was founded by the Phrygian hero Solimus and took its name from him. We have Ovid's word for it in Book IV of the *Fasti,* and while it is well to doubt the words of a historian, it is not advisable to doubt those of a poet:

> *Attulit Aeneas in loca nostra deos.*
> *Heius erat Solymus Phrigia comes unus ab Ida,*
> *A quo Sulmonis moenia nomen habent;*
> *Sulmonis gelidi, patriae, Germanice, nostrae.*

To console Ovid's sadness, the hurdy-gurdies play long into the night on the streets of Sulmona, and their notes fall like sonorous drops into a resonant lake. In Piazza XX Settembre, dominated at its center by the statue of the Poet, the window display of a candy store glitters. The monument, by Ettore Ferrari, is an exact replica of the statue erected in Rumania on the supposed site of the ancient Tomis. It is a decorous monument, despite the Art Nouveau flourishes flanking the lyre that adorns the base. Ovid wears a toga and is awaiting inspiration, a stylus in his hand and this hand raised to support his chin. *Pelignae decar gloria gentis ego.* Other confectioneries gleam in the adjacent streets, their windows displaying with childish charm crowns, baskets, braids, bunches of flowers, all of multicolored sugar. This too is an homage to Ovid, "poet of childhood."

The medieval aqueduct crosses the city like a huge worm, now in the open, now diving inside the houses. We take a look at the *membra disiecta* of San Francesco della Scarpa, which has its facade on one side and the portal on the other; we enter the Casa della Santissima Annunziata, and there, at the back of the entrance hall, stuck to the wall and suspended in mid-air, we find Ovid in his Second Life, wearing a doctoral tunic, with the grave look and wrinkles around the mouth of a man who has lived much, a short cloak around his neck, and his left foot resting on a book. And when we ask our guide why Ovid should have books under his feet, she replies that Ovid was so learned that he read "even with his feet."

It is night when we leave Sulmona. The statue of Ovid descends from its pedestal and follows us with great bronze footsteps. So as to quicken his pace, the poet grasps his toga with both hands and pulls it up above his knees. Thus girded, Publius Ovidius Naso resembles the ladies of 1905, who lifted their skirts when crossing muddy streets.

Ettore Ferrari cast his statue of Ovid with the bronze from German cannons. The symbolic meaning of this casting does not coincide with what we know of Ovid's warlike sentiments. In the first book of the *Ars Amatoria,* the poet sings of the rape of the Sabines and concludes as follows: "You alone, O Romulus, were able to give such opportunities to soldiers. Give them to me as well, and I too will be a soldier." "*Haec mihi si dederis commoda, miles ero.*" For the statue's height and build, the sculptor was inspired by the Marane peasants, who live in a hamlet near the Fountain of Love and are very tall and brawny.

The statue is gaining on us. Not for nothing, however, have gangster films been shown on our screens. Concezio puts out the lights and stops the automobile on a side road. The bronze footsteps come close to us, then fade in the direction of Corfinio. The road on which we have stopped is the one leading to the Abbey of the Celestines.

Pietro di Angelerio from Isernia felt himself destined for a hermit's life, and to reinforce his calling took up his abode in the most remote caves in the mountains of Abruzzo. One day, along with two devoted companions, Pietro climbed the Majella in search of a refuge there, but the place was so frightening that the two companions turned back and left their future pope to himself. It was in his refuge on the Majella that Pietro battled the Tempter and overcame him, after which he descended to the plain and at the foot of Mount Morrone founded the Celestine Abbey. It was 1241.

The road becomes rough and narrows to a path. A head pops up out of the bushes, and we stop to ask the direction of the Abbey, but the recipient of the question, whether out of aphonia or stupidity, looks at us without answering. While the automobile is getting started again, a second head pops up and immediately disappears, but not before we have had time to recognize it as a woman. Ovid's art of metamorphosis has been somewhat forgotten in these parts, but in compensation the art of love is studied with much zeal.

To found his Abbey, Pietro began with the enlargement of an ancient chapel named for the Virgin, and next to it built a church dedicated to the Holy Spirit. Here Brother Pietro founded the Celestine order, at first placed by Urban IV under the Rule of Saint Benedict, and later set up with its own rules and hierarchy by the General Council of Lyons in 1274.

The obstacles in our path increase. The automobile turns into a ship and the road into the Sargasso Sea. The floating seaweed is actually a dense mass of men, women, and children lying dimly on the ground in interlaced positions. Our vehicle cuts its way laboriously across this carpet of flesh, while they shift feebly, like sleepers turning over in their sleep. It is obvious that we are going through inhabited places, though there are still none of those fires that mark inhabited places and determine their importance. A local song says about ancient Corfinium that " *'n tiempe de' gentile, faceva fòcora cientemile*" ("in pagan times it had a hundred thousand hearths"). We yell from the windows — is this the right road for the Abbey? — and from that mattress of human seaweed come voices that could just as well mean "yes" as "no," and indeed are not so much sounds meant to convey ideas as moans of suffering or love. "I asked you in vain, O night, devoid of sight and devoid of pity."

Around the year 1299, Charles II of Anjou exalted the Morrone Abbey so that it became one of the most notable buildings in the kingdom. When the Celestine Order was suppressed in 1807, the Abbey was first assigned to the Collegio dei Tre Abruzzi, then used as a workhouse, and finally as a penitentiary.

"Pelos brings luck" say the dream books, written for people who play the lottery. Just as Concezio utters the word "penitentiary," the beam of our headlights strikes an obstacle that looms up out of the night: the single, massive, impenetrable door of the prison.

The suppression of the Celestines caused grave damage. The land around here is extremely fertile and every clod of earth is a breast, but what for us is metaphor, in the time of the Celestines was reality. They had hauled lead pipes up to the top of Mount Morrone, and from up there irrigated these lands with milk. During the Great War, the Abbey was filled with Austrian prisoners, and they, to keep their proverbial culture fresh, sacked the splendid library assembled during centuries of patience by the Celestine fathers.

The church, in the form of a Greek cross, is also reduced to considerable squalor, although the magnificent organ built in 1681 by the Milanese Gian Battista del Frate survives. As for the paintings in the Caldora Chapel, attributed to Leonardo da Teramo, they look more like old geographical maps than frescoes illustrating the Holy Scriptures. From vast empty spaces, a head sometimes emerges, or an arm, or a halo. But at night, the Christ painted by Master Leonardo opens his eyes and pricks up his ears. In the dark and silent countryside a voice is heard. It is like a star that instead of falling from the sky on the earth, rises from the earth to the sky. And calls: "O Alfredo . . ." Whereupon, from the depths of the penitentiary, a man's voice, muffled, hollow, lost in the distance, answers: "O Mariantonia . . ."

Christ turns to those who stand behind him. "I know better than anyone how great the sins of men are, having become man in order to redeem them, but they do not justify the horror of punishment."

An old man with a Semitic nose and curly beard, whom Master Leonardo has painted to the right of the Lord, objects: "Yet prison is simply a mild anticipation of Hell."

Christ flies into a rage. "I did not invent Hell. Every teacher is the victim of his own disciples and their foolish interpretations. The same thing happened to Wagner, to Nietzsche, to Picasso. Hell existed long before me. The Persians had it, the Chaldeans, the Egyptians, the Greeks. And they transmitted it to the Etruscans, and they to the Romans. In the end it was adopted by the Christians too. But not all the Fathers of the Church accept the absurd belief in eternal punishment. In 1761, the Huguenot Petit-Pierre published an admirable little book on the 'non-everlastingness of punishment,' which is a metaphysical prelude to Cesare Beccaria's treatise on temporal punishment."

Christ's anger will surprise only those who know the conventional Christ of the catechisms but are ignorant of the Christ who at the age of thirty withdrew into the proud scorn of one "who is not understood," and spent the last three years of his life in bitter solitude.

"Alfredo . . . !" the prisoner's woman repeats in the night. Christ's face darkens with melancholy. "Why bother to discuss these things? Let us return to the rigidity and silence given us by the good Leonardo da Teramo, and wait for the saltpeter on this wall to end by effacing even our shadow." The light in Christ's eyes goes out, his ears settle back, and in the cold silence of the church Gian Battista del Frate's organ gives forth a desolate cadenza.

The Celestine Abbey has the look of a fortress. We drive around behind the impregnable structure, since from the directions given to us in a nearby tavern, clearly used by the prison guards for quenching their thirst, it is on that side that we will find the road leading to the Fountain of Love. At Mont Saint-Michel in Normandy we had also been struck by this sinister affinity between Abbey and Prison. The walls are painted pink, but is a coat of paint enough to compensate for the lack of air, light, and freedom? Our senses not only signal things to us, but give them new form in accordance with our inclinations and mood. Tonight pink is to us the color of death.

This road is even rougher than the one we took to get to the Abbey. Under the glare of our headlights, a hunter stops near the bushes to let us pass. He carries his gun slung across his shoulder and holds his dog by the ears. Concezio asks him if he can sell us some game, but he replies that he is not a hunter, adding in a low voice, "I work for the penitentiary." We leave him behind, one who in the night ambushes not birds or hares but quite another kind of game, and in a short while we recognize a hollow in the ground as the Fountain of Love.

A row of poplars forms a semicircle behind the two fountains: the old and the new. The latter is dedicated to Victory and bears the date 1919. All that remains of the ancient one is a small dry ruin, on which we read this odd inscription: "Princess Infantry Regiment A. D. 1883." Under the inscription is a whitish rectangle from which a plaque has obviously been pried loose.

"The plaque said it was by this fountain that Ovid used to meet Corinna at night."

These words are spoken by a tall youth, wearing gray pants and a striped jersey, and holding a horse by the bit. The horse bends to drink slowly, silently, and — supreme elegance — without showing a sign of pleasure. In the youth with the striped jersey we recognize one of the Dioscuri, but which of the two we don't know.

"Does Ovid still come to this fountain?"

"He still wanders around these parts, sometimes as a friar, sometimes as a poodle dog, sometimes in the form of a wheel of fire."

Another youth has answered, having arrived in the meantime, he too dressed, as happens with brothers, in a pair of gray pants and a striped jersey. He holds a bicycle by the handlebars and pushes it toward the fountain to water it. The Dioscuri are partially up-to-date, and now one is a trainer of horses, the other of bicycles.

"A painter friend of ours," we tell them, "depicted you as handsome young men but completely black, because in his great innocence he had discovered that Dioscuri means *dii oscuri*, 'dark gods.' Etymology is the siren of simple minds."

The two youths look at us with the uncertain smile of those who haven't understood, and the one with the horse says, "We're too young to know much about Ovid, but if you'll come up here to the Marane, you'll find some old people who know a lot more about him than we do."

Castor and Pollux place themselves one on our right and the other on our left, and like suspects arrested by the carabinieri we set off into the night.

San Giovanni in Venere, 19 August

Gabriele d'Annunzio is addressing the ghost of Mario Bianco, killed in the capture of Tripoli:

> Dear boy, if here you neither hear
> the din of battle nor are sated by
> the blood shed by brave men after you,
>
> Here, buried in the grace of San Giovanni,
> well you hear your hollow oaks
> prophesying to the wind of Dalmatia.

The image of the "hollow oaks" has adhesive qualities and sticks in the memory of the friend who is driving us on this journey in Abruzzo. While the automobile covers the short, straight road leading from Fossacesia to San Giovanni in Venere, Concezio repeats the d'Annunzian image *sotto voce* and slowly savors it.

Others call the automobile *macchina,* machine, but I do not like the pretentiousness of this figure. Between machine and automobile there is as much difference as between a greyhound and an ordinary dog. I prefer the ordinary dog.

We arrive in San Giovanni in Venere in late morning, and even before taking a look at the basilica, we examine the trunks of the oaks that on the right, and in the company of some olive trees, go to make up a small forest. *Not one of them is hollow.*

San Giovanni in Venere stands high above the sea. Up here man feels the grandeur of nature more keenly.

We advance to the edge of the small plateau. One's gaze finds no obstacles, and the lungs expand to the breath of the infinite.

But beware! In this sublime atmosphere there is the risk of becoming stupid. Man should live in small, low rooms, and either not look at the sky at all or look at it through very narrow windows.

Perhaps we misunderstood. But what can "hollow oak" mean if not oak "split by lightning"? For many, poetry is sublime imprecision. In our urge to verify, some may have thought they saw an a-poetical sentiment. Meanwhile, as a result of these ambiguities, the cards of poetry lie in great confusion. Goethe would have said *poetry and truth,* and this is one of the few reasons why we have not stopped paying our respects to the "Olympian" Wolfgang.

Lightning loves oak trees. At Dodona, on the Campidoglio in Rome, in the Romowe in Prussia, great honors were paid to this friend of lightning. For the ancients, the place struck by lightning, which the Greeks called *enelusio* and the Romans *fulguritum,* was sacred and full of blinding divinity. Even today the Greek peasant who passes near a "hollow" oak crosses himself, and men and beasts struck by lightning without fatal consequences are allowed to rest and live out their days without working.

The oaks of San Giovanni are full, round, and intact. Such immunity is surprising and worrisome. Does Jove never come this way?

This oak grove is noble. Worthy to guard the weapons of a hero, like that small wood in Thessaly in which Hercules' club was placed, along with his lion skin. The only danger up here is Wagnerism, verbose and beautiful stupidity.

Not only Jove, but even the lesser divinities, the *volaille céleste,* do not frequent this place. A great solitude surrounds the basilica, a vast silence. The grass is scanty and strewn with bits of pottery. A cart that had been transporting bricks has stopped work, and horse and driver have retired to the brief shade between the curve of the apse and the beginning of the nave. This basilica was built in the seventh century on the ruins of a temple of Venus the Conciliatrix, and dedicated to Saint John the Evangelist. Inside, in a shabby notebook on a wretched little table near a pillar, one reads: "Basilica of S. Giovanni in Venere, built on the ruins of the temple of Venus the Conciliatrix by the monk Martinus in the years 529-543, 6th century of Christ." We are always disturbed by the cohabitation of saints and pagan deities, and especially this one between the youngest of the apostles and the goddess of love and beauty. What will they have to say to each other? What is their attitude toward each other? If we, who are not saints, feel such awkwardness at finding ourselves alone with a woman, just imagine him, the author of the Apocalypse! And with such a woman! And the two of them alone up here, in conversation with the wind and stars! It's true that in his mortal life John went through much worse. Arriving in Rome, under the reign of Nero, he was plunged three times into a cauldron of boiling oil, and three times he emerged from it unscathed, while others would have been turned into fritters. And besides between John and Venus a deep rivalry prevails. Never will enmity prove to be so useful to someone "who accepts no excuses."

In the light a voice calls, "Giovanni!" But when we turn around, there is no one there.

The cloister is to the left of the basilica, and behind it lie peaceful trenches where a few stumps of columns sprout like asparagus. Other stumps, along with their drums, are scattered in the grass of the cloister. In the portico framing the cloister a dentist has been at work. Signs of the prothesis are visible everywhere, especially in the mullioned windows restored with cement, that plebeian among construction materials.

"Did you hear?" Concezio exclaims, and as he turns completely around, he slaps himself on the neck, as though to drive away a horsefly.

Was it Venus or was it John? To resolve this doubt, one would have to wait for evening, when in the shadows the luminous forms are rekindled of the saint and the goddess, who now pass by invisibly, brush against us, and breathe their presence in our faces. For forty consecutive days, at the end of each night, the Christians of Palestine saw, and the pagans saw too, the New Jerusalem foretold in the Apocalypse, which little by little took shape in the air and shone like a city of sugar;

then, gradually as day broke, faded and disappeared in the light. Will we, in this solitude swarming with mystery, will we have the patience to wait for nightfall?

The custodian of the basilica emerges from the little door of the sacristy. He is young and sick. He is also like John, an apostle fleeing from Calvary. But the apostles fleeing from Calvary, where do they go today? It is obvious that the clothes he is wearing were not cut to his size. They may have been given to him in some house in Fossacesia. The lady of the house would have said to him, "I can't give you any money, my good man, but take this jacket of my husband's, it's almost new." The custodian comes toward us, dragging his feet, his knees wobbly. The wind from the sea ruffles the sparse hair on the top of his head. The shadow of his beard extends the shadow that descends from his flushed cheekbones. His face is bloodless, his eyes downcast and expressionless. He is indifferent, absent, remote. Weak as they are, his eyes pierce us and look beyond us at the "hollow" oaks, the sea, the sky. Concezio's presence might save us from embarrassment, but Concezio, huge and light on his feet, nimble as a butterfly hunter, is prancing around the basilica and taking pictures.

The custodian stops as though to let someone pass, then turns to follow whoever it is with his eyes. He certainly sees "them" even by day, and if his eyes are blank, it is because they have been burned by this light in the light.

We enter the basilica, hurrying our step, but everything has been cleared out before we arrive. Nothing is left. And so that there would be even less, they have given the walls a coat of raw umber, by way of restoration. "To isolate the older parts," the custodian explains. As though a woman were to have a beautiful nose and they painted the rest of her face with raw umber.

If they have not also taken away this little dry and dusty holy-water stoup, it is because the holy-water stoup is built into the pillar. On the wall of the apse, to the left of the main altar, a few pale figures emerge from under the coat of raw umber. The frescoes driven back by the restoration are trying to come forward again. We see two pupils staring fixedly in the effort, elbows and fists extended; and when we go closer we hear the muffled whimpers, the panting of these figures struggling to free themselves. Does anyone pay attention to such signs? Great is the vitality of the painted figures, and very great their power. What can this stupid, neutral layer of paint do against such strength? Soon the last resistance will be broken, and in the impetus of liberation saints and warriors will leap out of the wall and roll pell-mell in the middle of the deserted basilica.

From John's church we descend into the Cyprian's temple. Squat green columns support the low ceiling, and the effort has eroded the capitals. Christ is seated above the sacrificial altar. Even in the choice of votive animals — doves and lambs — there is an affinity of tastes. Splintered candlesticks, a prie-dieu, a broken mannequin (why a painter's mannequin in a church?), and some plaster saints are heaped in a storeroom. One of them prays with his eyes to heaven and his hands joined. Passing next to him, we whisper, "Get some rest!" but he goes on praying. You can see that it's all he knows how to do.

A little barefoot girl tags along behind the custodian, holding a rag doll with her right hand, and with her left a tiny little brother with a naked bottom. The baby wants the doll and bursts into tears. His wailing swells in the basilica, and the emptiness exaggerates it.

The pronaos is terraced. The facade is bare. Around the portal there are still a few squat sculptures, with the faces of idiots, like certain statues produced by sculptors today. That this should be the tradition? Olive trees, oaks, cypresses, and pines are scattered around the edges. The air is full of an incessant hum.

A crypt opens under the pronaos. A strong smell of human excrement stops us on the threshold, but there in the depths something is shining. If "they" do not smell this fetid odor, it is because the immortals live beyond suffering and stenches. Hidden behind a pillar, we can watch them at our ease. John preserves a kind of romantic air about him and looks like Chopin. Venus has arrived at the age of *Maman Colibri.* She still makes love but she doesn't tire you out, and if you have a tummyache she'll make you a cup of camomile tea.

Venus asks:

"And that friend of yours, the one you called 'master'?"

John replies:

"I don't know. We're all waiting for him. But who knows if he'll come in time . . . ."

Charun said: "You've rested enough. Come along now, and I'll take you to my country."

Cerveteri, 2 September

After leaving Rome and following the Via Aurelia, we come to the 41-kilometer stone and the turn-off to the right that leads to the necropolis of Cerveteri.

Caere was one of the oldest and most powerful cities of the dodecapolis, the Etruscan confederation of twelve cities extending between the right bank of the Tiber and the barrier of the Apennines. To make something memorable it used to be customary to give it a Greek name, and the Greeks in their turn gave the city of Caere a Phoenician name and called it Agylla.

It is an Etruscan principle, and proof of great wisdom, that the sea is kept at a distance. At Cerveteri too, as at Tarquinia, the sea is a backdrop for the landscape. From the fact that the most important Etruscan cities, with the sole exception of Populonia, lay inland, it has been argued that the Etruscans came to Italy overland. Is the spirit of the wayfarer less adventurous, less poetic, less inclined to great deeds and sublime aspirations? Just as marriage kills love, so does navigation destroy the love of the sea. The way the sea is placed on the borders of Etruscan cities reveals a knowledge of indirect effects, a deep and subtle feeling for decoration, a "marine shrewdness," such as we do not find in more properly maritime peoples. For seaports, Caere had at its disposal Alsium (today Palo) and Pyrgi, today called Santa Severa.

Something mysterious happened in the thirteenth century: the people of Caere were seized by an unconquerable aversion for their city, abandoned it *en masse,* and moved seven kilometers eastward, to Caere Novum, beyond the Fosso Sanguinara. Whoever said that thirteen was lucky? Even the names of these places arouse thoughts of death. The old city remained deserted and in the condition of a skeleton, like the carcass of a locust on a tree in autumn, and from *Caere vetus* came to be called Cerveteri.

Death, death, death.

The top of the Topolino is down, and to the charming companion seated beside me, who has pulled up her skirt in order to take the sun on her magnificent legs, I am careful not to confess the mysterious terror that all of a sudden casts a shadow on my heart.

The attraction of death is irresistible. It is for this reason that men build civilizations, and each time with infinite patience start rebuilding them all over again. Civilization is a game, a distraction, the most effective way we have of banishing the thought of death from our minds. It deludes us with its ideas of progress, of goals to be achieved, of destiny to be fulfilled, and meanwhile it leads us into a futile and heedless life: a life *that does not allow us to think of anything else.* Why do men in cities walk in such a hurry? To escape the thought of death. And from the moment they awaken until they go to sleep, their lives are completely covered over with occupations, useless in themselves but necessary so as to leave no holes through which the horrible thought might insinuate itself. Even the etiquette books, those guides for the civilized person, advise you not to talk about death in polite society.

Another way to overcome the thought of death is to face up to it and make it your chief occupation in life. This is the "Etruscan" way. Even the evil eye, say the experts, can be neutralized by resolutely confronting the one who casts it.

So far we have followed the great secure and shining highway, measured at intervals by milestones and marked along its sides by small white cubes, heading in the direction of such large and successful cities as Genoa and Turin, a road glowing with the fascination of the West, and on which one constantly meets, or passes, or is passed by other automobiles coming from every part of Italy and the world.

One may also cross the ocean, but on the route laid out by the shipping companies, and on which at night one meets luxury liners illuminated like theaters.

But at the 41-kilometer stone, we leave the route of luxury liners and of automobiles that carry radio antennas on their roofs, and fling outselves into desert seas and toward unknown islands. The only vehicle we meet is a hooded gig with a family dangling out of it, and the children look at us with two black moons motionless in the middle of a white sky. Over us fly huge, heavy, featherless birds, made only of gray and leaden flesh, and on this land consecrated to death, their shadows pass like the shadows of airplanes.

Desert seas and unknown islands . . . Cerveteri is an island surrounded by a sea of barren lands. It is rocky and austere, supported on all sides by enormous rusty walls, and dominated by a large castle reinforced at its corners by round towers.

Towers have the same function in castles as padded shoulders in jackets.

Cerveteri did not begin to make a comeback until the fifteenth century, under the rule of the Orsini family, then of the Farnese, then once again the Orsini, and finally the Ruspoli, owners of this great palace with its square plan and cylindrical towers, which plays the part of padded shoulders over old Caere.

Cerveteri is not easily approachable, and one can see why, at the time of the invasion by the Gauls in 390 B.C., it was chosen as a place of refuge for the vestal virgins and the sacred treasures of Rome.

In the spacious courtyard of the Palazzo Ruspoli, hunters and horse dealers are gathered around the drinking trough. The horses drink with a dignity that even the most well brought-up man would be unable to match. The horse dealers move awkwardly, like dismounted centaurs. As men accustomed to looking into the distance, they carry their heads high. Summer has reduced them to idleness, but on dark evenings in winter, the season of their glory, they return to the city, bent under the wind, and hole up inside the Osteria dei Cacciatori, the tavern close by in Piazza Risorgimento, near the wall fountain where the women of Cerveteri are now drawing water in gleaming copper pans, and from their belts they unload the huge, heavy, and featherless birds that a short while ago we saw pass over the countryside like ravens over the corpse of Siegfried, and which they have downed after a bitter struggle, marked on their faces and hands by deep and bloody furrows.

Man in these parts continues to dig his dwelling place in the tufa, the craftsman runs his workshop in the walls of ancient Caere, and the ironmonger, the blacksmith, and the carpenter attend to their daily tasks hidden inside these masses of stone, which their ancestors piled up twenty-five centuries ago, when their city was at war with Rome and the Tarquins returned to take shelter among the original rocks.

The visit to the tombs is free, the only requirement being that the visitor sign a register.

Why should it be free? With the proceeds from selling entrance tickets they could resume the excavations interrupted five years ago (out of the total area of the necropolis of 350 hectares, only sixteen have been excavated), and at the same time it would give satisfaction to the Etruscans, who considered death as a highly important and decorous condition of life.

This insistence on making us sign puts us on our guard. What duties are we incurring? Everyone must sign: I, my companion, who in the meantime has pulled down her skirt, and my daughter Angelica, a first-year pupil in the *ginnasio*, who composes a masterly signature in the register, rounding the tail of the A like a conch shell.

"What about him?" asks the custodian, pointing to my son Ruggero.

Ruggero is four and a half years old, and I feel no shame in admitting that he is still illiterate. But my answer does not persuade the custodian. So he's illiterate, and why should an illiterate be allowed to enter the city of the Etruscan dead without signing?

An advocate of symbols, the custodian considers the signature as a form of payment, and this new Charon is asking for the symbol of a symbol. Guided by the hand of his daddy, Ruggero's tiny hand traces in the register the diagram of a distant earthquake.

The register sits in a little room whose door and windows are protected by metal screens, under a chromolithograph showing Victor Emmanuel III at the time he was Prince of Naples, next to a bookshelf enclosed by wire netting, in which a number of periodicals of Etruscan archaeology are lined up in their gray covers. Their appearance is that poor and naked one that Petrarch saw in Philosophy. In our honor, the custodian dons his jacket and puts his cap on his head. An ancient catarrh, obviously of Etruscan origin, racks his bronchial tubes and forces him to spit frequently.

On the threshold of this necropolis to which I have come with the firm determination of seeing, and for whose sake I have endured a long and tiring journey, my strength fails me and my will recedes. I do not recall such an aversion to anything since the dark years of childhood, a day when my father and I, after a long horseback ride under the sun in an Eastern desert country, descended into an underground cistern, guided by a kind of palikar wearing a fustanella, who preceded us with a resin torch. To the eye, the water in that cistern, as devoid of surface as of depth, revealed itself only by the flashing reflections of the torch, but its stench of a liquid corpse made me so giddy that I kept staggering on the slippery steps, until a soft splash, perhaps the dive of a water snake, dissolved all my resistance and I fell into the arms of the palikar, who smelled of goat cheese.

Turn back! But where will I get the courage to overcome the "official" shame that makes us commit so many acts contrary to our wishes? Luckily for me, the custodian has noticed nothing, because except for the mortuary customs of the Etruscans, the mind of this ghost-watcher is obscured by dense clouds. He looks at me mutely and waits for me to pass, for resolute as he was in denying me entrance to the necropolis until I had signed the register, he is equally resolute, now that I have signed, in not letting me leave without having first descended among the tombs.

Among the tombs . . .

A fine way to behave for a man *who has seen worse.* You feel yourself being stirred like minestrone by a ladle when they tell you that the ruts in this tufa road, on which you set your feet shod in cow leather, were dug three thousand years ago by the carts that transported the horizontal bodies of the inhabitants of Caere adorned with their weapons and all their riches, and from time to time that of a Lucumon.

Once again the metaphysics of the comic arrive just in time to mitigate the metaphysics of the tragic: at the sound of the word Lucumon, along comes the similarity to the word *loukoum,* Turkish delight. Laughter makes a man strong.

The Etruscans are our romantic fathers. The stubborn fury by which Rome sought to disperse the Etruscans, destroy their civilization, and silence their language was inspired by its inborn aversion to any sort of romanticism. The struggle between Romans and Etruscans was more than a war of religion: it was a war of souls. Rome prevailed, but something of the romantic Etruscan soul remained, like a thin cloud in the metallic sky of Rome. It is that slender romantic vein that runs through our poetry, now inspiring Virgil to write his Fourth Eclogue, now dictating to Petrarch the first sonnet of the *Canzoniere,* now suggesting to Raphael his Saint Peter in prison, now singing to Bellini the "Cari Luoghi" from *La Sonnambula:* a touch of melancholy in the midst of so much serenity, a shadow of the past in the midst of so much present.

The romantic soul is horizontal, the classical soul vertical. The romantic soul is centrifugal, the classical soul centripetal. The romantic soul desires what it doesn't have and tends to detach itself from reality and even from the earth, the classical soul is unaware of the wish and replenishes itself. And if we do not apologize for the simplistic nature of these comparisons, it is because we like such simplification and believe that, in addition to laughter, simplification also makes a man strong.

Without the traces left in us by the subtle poisons of the Etruscans, their acute doubts, their metaphysical terrors, our souls would be pure but without drama, like music made by vocalizing alone, and incapable of consonant voices, harmonies and disharmonies, symphonic composition and universality.

Marching at the head of the alphabetic army, "the" vowels are the militiamen of classicism, with the romantic soldiery of the consonants following along behind. A classical language and one of song, Italian boasts the musicality of its "AEIOU-ism." Someone has attributed the clipped pronunciation of English to the fog that forces you to keep your mouth closed. Is this explanation really all that "unphilological"? So then why do we think "more clearly" in the dark? Even among languages, there are some that are more modest and veiled, which prefer to say less than they are thinking and like to approach silence.

Oddly enough, in the older Etruscan the vowels prevailed and the union of two consonants was avoided. Here is an inscription found on a vase in Caere: *minice umamina umaramlistae ipurenaie eeraisieepana minenunastavhelefu.* You can see that, aside from swallowing a fly, there could not have been much danger in keeping one's mouth open in Etruria.

Then, little by little, the Etruscan language begins to lose its vowels, to extinguish its lights and veil itself. Minerva becomes *Menrva,* Alexander *Elchsentre.* After which one can better understand certain contractions of dialect, and why the people of Parma call their city *Perma,* and those of Genoa call theirs *Zena.* But why speak of the corruption and coarsening of Etruscan? It elevates itself to its own "desire for mystery," perfects itself, becomes subtle and enriched with allusions; and does not the attitude of someone who has something to hide attract us much more than one whose chest is transparent, eye free of secrets, and brow occupied with nothing more than the present? Besides, it is well for language and religion to resemble each other, and a "speculative" religion like the Etruscan would have clashed with an open language that said *everything with the first sound.* It was not a single paradise that hung above the heads of the Etruscans, but a celestial "double background," and "the world with its gods was lorded over by the veiled gods, who were held accountable by Tinia himself, the Etruscan Jove."

There was a "Faustian" soul in these romantics of our ancient world, and who knows if, in rending the veil that covers their language, there might not spill forth such sounds as to overturn our whole literary heritage and stain its golden monuments forever?

It was not for their physical strength that the Etruscans were frightening, but for the strength of their secrets, for what they persisted in leaving unsaid. They had every right to be called "witnesses." And since the gods are made in the image of men, and not men in the image of the gods, the Etruscan gods were cruel and malign, because so were the Etruscans themselves.

Their cults were especially cruel. Phocaean prisoners were butchered at Caere, and to find bloody ceremonies to match, we would have to cross the ocean and go among the Incas. But there is something stronger in the Etruscans: there is the possibility of overcoming death, there is redemption. And who knows if the Romans' aversion for the Etruscans was not the prelude to their aversion for the Christians?

Malignity and cruelty glitter in the Etruscan's slanting eyes, in his wolfish smile. It is the smile of one who knows he is hitting others while he himself is invulnerable.

We see the Etruscans dead. We see them reclining on their sarcophagi, pairs of faithful spouses. But if they should get to their feet, we would see them launch themselves all together, jerking like electrocuted frogs, to the rhythm of heels stamping the ground and the double leap, into the Polovetsian dances from *Prince Igor*. When we think of the Etruscans, we hear the music of Borodin.

Cruelty and malignity are followed by lesser faults: a taste for the absurd, distortion of reality, reversal of values, "black humor," magianism, surrealism, the whole diabolical game that fills the world of *metaphysica naturalis*.

To these metaphysicians and the danger they represented, Rome opposed its own logic, the *health* of its own logic, for in Rome's action there was a certain apostolicism. The enemy of all diversity, of all possibility of diversity, logic is the only science that can provide any assurance of good here on earth.

Between logicians and metaphysicians there is no possibility of compromise. Rome vanquished the Etruscans, and strove with particular pertinacity to obscure their language, the instrument that propagated their dangerous fantasies (we reserve the word "ideas" for what has a sure philosophic value). And it succeeded so well that still today Etruscan is a closed language.

Who will open up this language and how? The most recent "key" is the one that presupposes a strict kinship between Etruscan and Hebrew and proceeds by comparisons between these two languages. What is the truth? We have no way of judging. But the inventor of this "key" was a priest named Tarquini, and even without believing in the transcendental value of coincidences, one cannot deny that there is something "Etruscan" in this system.

There remain the "mysteries" hidden within this closed language. Pythagoras too is surrounded by mystery. Speaking of him in a handbook on the history of philosophy composed for his personal use, Schopenhauer shows a deep distrust for those who have left no written documents. We cannot say why, but we extend this distrust as well to things written *but indecipherable.* And we dread the day when they will be revealed. Leave the doors closed.

Cerveteri, 3 September

The usual decoration of cemeteries is not lacking in the necropolis of Cerveteri: urns are placed along the sacred way beside the tombs, and from them protrude the deformed stalks of rosebushes. Although when it comes to flowers, I share the sentiments of my friend Apollinaire:

> *j'aime les fruits, je déteste les fleurs,*

I recognize that this double row of flowering rosebushes must be a pleasant sight. But in this season the blossoms are gone, and it is distressing to see their skeletons, black and looking as though they had been pulled from a fire, drooping from the ends of the stems. The live vegetation consists of dwarf cypresses and panic grass, lighted up here and there by yellow broom. Tumuli rise from the earth like breasts, and the flora that covers them has not only a decorative but a utilitarian function, for it shores up these constructions with its roots and holds them firm. A triple groove gouged in the tufa forms a spiral edge around the tumuli. Each tumulus makes you think of a huge, half-buried top.

The most frightening thing about death is the idea of solitude. If the dead had voices, we would hear them cry at night from their distant prison: "Don't leave us alone! Don't leave us alone!" Religions have tried to "furnish" this void, but the fear of solitude has nevertheless remained.

Not everyone likes paradise. Apart from the sorting-out that will take place among us, some having to descend to hell, others going to purgatory, and still others rising to paradise, the life we are promised in the beyond is too different from our own, and does not correspond to the idea we have created for ourselves of a stable and final dwelling place.

There is "functionalism" in the life of the beyond; it lacks domestic warmth. What we want is not a blessed life, but a life similar to this one that we are accustomed to, and which we like.

We want to go on the same way.

One goes away for the pleasure of coming back. But to go away without coming back, or else to regions where nothing guarantees us the usual company, the loves we have acquired with so much effort, so much patience, and which now surround us like petals surrounding the pistil?

Great psychologists of death, the Etruscans understood that it was best to dismiss any idea of transubstantiation — which I too dismiss, if only so as not to have to pronounce this unbearable word — and keep home and family the way they are down here.

If the family is the origin of the State, it is hard to understand why the Etruscans, whose family life was so strong and compact, gradually slackened as their society expanded, and ended up weak and disunited within their confederation.

These "romantic fathers" of ours built houses, and little by little cities, to live in eternally when they were dead. They dug them in tufa because this was their custom for the houses of the living, and because the house dug in stone gives greater assurance of solidity, even if dug in a stone as soft as tufa.

No material was brought to their necropoli; everything was built with material found on the site. This, too, is a form of "autochthonism," which in the Etruscans was a mania. Men and things were supposed to die in the place where they were born. Isn't it curious that the first idea of the noble should be immobility?

To give form and decorum to this mania of theirs, the Etruscans conceived the fable of Tages or Tarchies, in its original sound, the "god born from clods." This god was unearthed near Tarquinia by a peasant's plow. He revealed to the Etruscans the science of thunderbolts, and immediately died. To put it more accurately, he went back under the clods, like someone who sticks his head out from under the bedsheets, gives the maid her instructions for the day, then burrows under the covers again. For the rest of his days, that peasant was left paralyzed and mute. This is what you get for seeing a god.

Lightning is the element dominating the Etruscan religion, and the most important religious prescriptions were contained in the *libri fulgurales.* The reason is obvious. Etruscan cities were built on high ground, under a dark, dense sky, streaked with lightning in zig-zag, ladder, and shuddering patterns, all of which converged on the rooftops and towers of this wonder-struck and terrorized people.

In that dark, dense sky sat Tinia (Jove), Uni (Juno), and Menvra (Minerva). This triad in its turn formed part of an ennead, and to this ennead were added three more gods to complete the group of twelve *Di Consentes;* and higher, and again in threes, sat the *Di Involuti* or veiled gods, whose faces no one, not even the gods of the first triad, had ever seen.

The Romans were struck by the hierarchy of this divine world, but did not understand why the Etruscans applied this hierarchy to their gods and not to themselves. As for faith in the number three and its multiples, which Plotinus carried into his philosophy and Dante into the *Divine Comedy,* and which we carry over into the order of our lives and work, it ran so deep in the Etruscans that cities that did not have three gates and three temples, or at least a single but tripartite temple, were considered "untrue."

What were all those gods arranged in threes doing up there? They were concerned with thunderbolts: the *Consentes* offered opinions on how to fabricate them, the *Involuti* taught how to launch them with the greatest possible effect, and Tinia, the beautiful god with goat's eyes and a blue beard, hurled them.

Tages, too, was a god, but ugly. He had a childish face and gray hair. Moreover he was a dwarf. This was to signify that Tages was old and at the same time a child, infantile and at the same time wise. In him, an old aspiration, thought to be unreachable, was actually reached: *"Si jeunesse savait, si vieillesse pouvait!"*

Despite the fright he gave the peasant who disinterred him, Tages was a little Benjamin Franklin for his humanitarian sentiments, and during his brief stay among the Etruscans he taught them how to draw down the threatening lightning, and how to bury it.

Mommsen treats this benefactor as a monster and speaks of him with horror. A strange reaction in one who should have brought to the examination of things of the past the indulgence, or at least the impassivity, that the doctor brings to the examination of corpses. But this historian *did not have a sense of the past,* and one day when Salomon Reinach showed him in the waters of Lake Garda near Salò the pile structures of lake dwellings rising from the bottom like colossal algae, Mommsen was dumbfounded. He had spent a lifetime studying Italy's past, but the thought that Italy had also undergone a lacustrine period had never occurred to him. It was a past too past for him.

Tages, the divine dwarf, combined in himself two ideas thought to be incompatible: youth and old age. Is this why Mommsen calls him a monster? Perhaps. People as a rule are unable to accept more than one idea at a time. Either young or old, but young and old at the same time, never!

The Etruscans built their first *"case da morto"** — puns are holy and in them we can recognize the voice of the gods — in the form of huts, with the roof narrower than

Case dei morti, houses of the dead / *casse da morto,* coffins. (Tr.)

the base and the walls leaning toward an ideal junction, like two hands joined in prayer. They were insignificant dwellings, suitable for deceased people of simple manners, and similar to the *caceretta* that the Lazio shepherd builds next to his hut, to store cheese. At the back of the tomb stood the sarcophagus of chestnut wood, surrounded by a ring of stones. Still today, in the Roman Campagna, they plant a wooden cross on the spot where a herdsman has died, and every passerby tosses a stone, which counts as a paternoster. Later the walls gradually straightened, the number of rooms increased to four, five, and six, and the *case da morto* held as many as fourteen horizontal tenants each.

The domes of these tombs look like bunkers sticking up from the ground, and invisible cannons are aimed against any eventual return of Tuchulcha, the frightful demon with ass's ears and beaked snout, who so tormented the poor Etruscans during their journey from the city of the living to the city of the dead. "Not a step farther!" Remember moving from the country house to a house in town, and from there to a building with four flats to the floor? In the time of my childhood, the prejudice resulting from such a move was still felt, and to live in an apartment was considered low class.

The same thing happened in the mortuary town planning of the Etruscans, where the one-family house gave way to phalansteries for several families and to so-called "sepulchral ways" that gave shelter to eighty dead arranged and laid out in rows. Among the living, the sepulchral ways were called "private streets."

The history of the Etruscans stopped, but had it continued, their necropoli today would bristle with skyscrapers, and the dead, decked out in fine garments embroidered with red thunderbolts, would go up and down on the elevators, except for the Lucumons, for whom, as persons of greater weight, the freight elevator would be reserved.

The necropolis was a continuation of the city, and man in dying had only to change his neighborhood, moving from the center of town to the more healthy and affluent suburbs.

The Etruscans did not confine the country of Utopia to inaccessible lands or remote islands, but to death, which is accessible to everyone. A highly sensible idea. The good order and happiness of families were now protected against all surprises, changes, and risks. Forever.

That the order and happiness of this ineffable citizenry are still intact is clear to us from the calm, the serenity, and this air of well-being that circulates hereabouts. Heavy masses of tufa, piled on top of one another, sealed the doors of these tombs for centuries; then Archaeology, in the person of Professor Mingarelli, the discoverer of this necropolis and now enjoying a well-deserved rest, one day opened the doors of the tumuli, and the dead slowly yawned, rubbed their eyes, and finally got out of their beds and went out for a stroll in the Via dell'Inferno, the main street of this city, and the lesser streets that branch off to right and left. These citizens, twenty-five centuries old, are invisible but present. If we pay close attention and cock an ear, we can hear the murmur of their packed and subdued voices.

And when a light breeze grazes our faces, it is one of them passing by.

Their speech is a twitter of birds. What are they saying? Etruscan is an obscure language, but here and there we can catch those few words that philology has revealed.

We hear *arakos,* which means vulture, and know that someone is talking about those heavy gray birds that just a while ago we saw pass over the countryside, spreading their large shadows on the earth like airplanes.

We hear *arimos,* and are sorry that a husband should call his wife a "monkey."

We hear *aguletora,* and also from the softer tone of voice we infer that a woman is speaking to a boy.

We hear *falado,* and are glad to know that a dead man is speaking of the sky . . . So we too, knowing he is watching us, lift our heads and look at the sky.

Then our gaze drops to the mountains, which from the Luparo to the Cerquino, Mount Pelato to Mount Spinesante, gradually slope to the boundless, empty sea.

This domestic peace and family sweetness are an invitation for when the time comes. What would we do in Paradise, we who are so easily bored and dislike the sound of treble voices and the organ? *Hic manebimus optime.* Here is a place for us as *paterfamilias,* and alongside it a place for our wife. We will ask her not to stay behind too long. She will not place herself on our right, as is our habit now, but on our left, like the day the two of us were married in church. And here are places for our children, to be left unoccupied as long as possible. But what will our Lina do with four places for servants? A single place is enough for her, unless she too, so young and deserving, gets married in the meantime and has children. But there will be room for everyone. Anyway, we will urge our good Lina not to join us before the year 2010. After all, beyond time, it's no trouble having to wait.

Likewise admirable is the administrative order of this city. Outside each tomb, a certain number of tufa cippi and small blocks, also of tufa, indicate how many men and how many women reside inside. Cippi and blocks are inserted in a common stone matrix, like phytin capsules in the perforated cardboard of the box. Wouldn't you say that the Porta San Paolo post office in Rome looks like an empty phytin box?

Occasionally, alongside the cippi and blocks, there is a cinerary urn. Cremation, which we once had the monstrous curiosity to witness through the peephole of a crematory oven, is the most horrible treatment that can be given a dead person.[1] But especially here in Cerveteri, where all the rest of the dead preserved their form, their home, and their habits, what was the point of being

---

1. The Catholic Church forbids cremation so that the deceased will find himself with his body intact on Judgment Day. But the Church burned heretics, a sign that it wanted to eliminate any possibility for those unfortunates likewise to present themselves at the sound of the last trumpet in the Valley of Jehoshaphat. What excessive cruelty! One might add that *mandati di cottura [mandati di cattura,* arrest warrants/*mandati di cottura,* "roast warrants" (Tr.)] had been issued for Giordano Bruno, Jan Hus, Etienne Dolet, etc.

reduced to a little heap of ashes? *Dummodo absolvar cinis . . .* But literary images, especially those inspired by the "vanity of all things," should not be taken literally.

Come, Maria, let's look for a home. It's nothing but an embarrassment of riches. How about this so-called Tomb of the Dolia, with its jars that once contained oil and cereals, and these balsam flasks in which you could put your lavender water, and these amphoras still full of wine tartar? Or would you be more comfortable in the Tomb of the Stuccoes, buried as it is beneath a magnificent oak, and guarded by this lion's head that looks as though it had been carved by Arturo Martini? In front of the Tomb of the Stuccoes one might stretch that canvas banner that I pointed out to you one day over a construction site in the Parioli quarter of Rome, on which was written: "Deluxe Apartments for Sale — *the Ultimate in Refinement.*" There's no lack of comfort. There's room for forty-eight persons. The beds for the head of the family and "his lady" are in an alcove; you go up three little steps and in the middle is the night table. And if these slippers you see at the foot of the bed are merely carved in bas-relief and painted in soft tempera colors, what difference does it make? The best life is the one reduced to symbols. And here is the cane for me and the fan for you. Look at the game bag for me, the hunter, and the mountain-climbing gear . . . But wait, there must be a mistake: I don't hunt and I don't climb mountains. And here's a little decanter for cognac, a shoemaker's knife, a saucepan, and a paddle for spreading the pasta. And here's an oar . . . Maria, we'll go rowing.

But what will we do with these paintings? What will

we do with this three-headed Cerberus, or this Typhon, whom our guide calls "siphon," and who with his serpent wound around his arm must be closely related to that double Typhon that I showed you in the little Acropolis museum in Athens, and who started staring at you with the black-rimmed eyes of a dirty old man, delightedly wagging his blue beard and long spiral tail? . . . We'll do what they do today with wall paintings: we'll scrape them.

"But maybe we'd be better off in the Tomb of the Little House, which has five rooms, six inside doors, and a small pantry at the back for foodstuffs."

"No," Maria replies. "The tenant of this tomb had two wives, and made them sleep in the same bed, while he selfishly slept in this other bed, alone. How about this next tomb instead, with its nice vestibule and apartments all around? Don't you like it?"

Now it's my turn to disagree: "No. In one of these little apartments there was a wife with two husbands, and to get them both in, that slut had the bed widened, as you can see, by adding more bricks."

We finally agree on the one that had been the tomb of Marce Ursus and his wife Ranta Prichin (the names are inscribed over the beds so you can't go wrong), and which in the wall between one room and another has two windows like railway ticket counters, so that neighbors can have a chat at night.

I ask the custodian, whom my companion with appropriate erudition calls Charun, i.e., Charon, what conditions must be met in order to be allowed to take up one's abode here when the time comes, and the custodian replies that all you have to do is to come with a little money in your pocket. This answer doesn't surprise me, and I remark to Charun that in many lands, for instance Abruzzo, it is still the custom to put a little money in the dead man's pocket; and Charun, in a variation on the same theme, adds that during the Great War, at the nearby airfield of Cerveteri, when a foreign aviator died, his comrades sent along with him not only money, but candies, chocolates, and even bottles of spumante.

We thank Charun and say goodbye with the hope of seeing each other again, but just as we emerge from the tomb of Marce Ursus and Ranta Prichin, we notice a small uncovered sarcophagus, not big enough for more than a six-month-old child.

"And who was this for?"

"Those were for children who didn't have the right to be inside the tombs."

What! All those comforts for the grownups, with beds, utensils, food, and the whole family warm and snug, with relatives and servants, and these poor little things outside here in the cold, with the rain and wind, and threatened by the terrible lightning?

This inhuman treatment surprises and pains us, and at the same time arouses our curiosity. For what reason, what lack of recognition, were these poor children kept outside the house?

Charun doesn't know.

At this point another question arises: does the malign influence exercised by the Tarquins in their lifetime still persist? No sooner are we out of the tomb named for this very old dynasty, and which along with the Tombs of the Sarcophagi, the Triclinium, and the Alcove, is one of the "outer" tombs of Cerveteri, than I stumble and sprain my ankle.

I am writing these pages reclining on the bed in the manner of the Etruscan spouses on the cover of the sarcophagus, and with a compress of vegetomineral water on my swollen ankle.

But the evil done by the Etruscans is cured by the Romans. Cato the Elder, being from Frascati, was as Roman as they come, and at the right moment we recall a highly effective saying of his for curing sprains (*De Re Rustica,* 160), which goes as follows:

"Hauat hauat hauat ista pista damia bodannaustra."

Tarquinia, 4 September

Unlike the well-furnished tombs of Cerveteri, those of Tarquinia are empty and uninhabitable. Where are the beds to stretch out on, the weapons for hunting, the games to play, the pans for roasting the little birds that lie on their backs with their claws contracted like the legs of racing cyclists? Where are the little windows between rooms for gossiping at night with the neighbors? Let's begin by saying that very few of these tombs have more than one room, and that even in death we would find the promiscuity of the common room intolerable.

In the tombs of Tarquinia, whose architecture is extremely poor when it exists at all, the representation of the world is entrusted solely to painting.

Nothing is more moving or consoling for us than this testimony that here on earth art alone is immortal, this mysterious instrument of what in ourselves is not mortal. It is a fine thing to live the life of the beyond in the midst of painting, as did the ancient dead of Tarquinia, but why not begin with that life, and live it in a world not real but painted, like the actors of former times in the midst of their stage sets? It would be much more civilized, more poetic, above all more human. What seas, what skies, what horizons, and what perspectives of architecture and streets! But stage sets have discarded the illusion of painting for "volumetric" reality. What an impoverishment! Perspectives are created by placing "volumes" one after another, no longer by carefully tracing lines on a flat surface that run into the distance and converge at an ideal point on the horizon, and by judiciously separating light and shadow. The miracle is relinquished and a heavy material substituted for a witty game. And this is only the least of it. Before we go any further, we are anxious to rid the idea of civilization of a gross misunderstanding: "mechanical" civilization is the exact opposite of civilization. The sad and stupid man watches with astonishment as the machine revolves, and its noise fills him with satisfaction.

In this respect the tombs of Tarquinia are "superior" to those of Cerveteri. Furnishings, conveniences, and all modern comfort are lacking, but there is this inner lining of painting that makes them so much more "open," so much more spirited!

The painting in the tombs of Tarquinia is very Greek. In the tombs closest to us in time, it is similar to the paintings in the Naples museum. Stendhal did not care for ancient painting. "We went to the Borgia apartments to see that ancient fresco, so celebrated in the eighteenth century under the title of the *Aldobrandini Wedding*. You will find much more important ancient frescoes in the Naples museum; they resemble Domenichino at his weakest. The *Wedding* gave us no pleasure." Stendhal was light and deep enough to understand the lightness and depth of Cimarosa and Raphael, but not enough to understand the lightness and depth of Greek painting. Not to mention the fact that the paintings in the Naples museum are not frescoes but encaustics. However much one may look with a pagan eye, as he did, at the Christian legend as illustrated by our painters, how heavy and debased it becomes when compared with the pagan legend! The first duty of painting is *to open a window on another world.* The Raphaels, Sebastiano del Piombos, and Michelangelo Anselmis in the painting gallery of the National Museum of Naples do not break this law, but try going from the rooms of the picture gallery to those in the same museum where wall paintings from the cities buried by Vesuvius are assembled, and you will see how the windows of the *Sacrifice of Iphigenia, Achilles and Chiron,* and *Cassandra Predicting the Downfall of Troy to Priam and Hector* open on spectacles much more remote from the drama of everyday life and absorbed in the aura of a lofty and at the same time gentle human poetry. The spectacles on which the "windows" in the tombs of Tarquinia open, however, are much more surprising, since in these hypogea one would expect dark underground scenes, and instead they are gazes directed at a most agreeable surface.

Many years ago, when I came to Tarquinia for the first time with Armando Spadini and Vincenzo Cardarelli, *civis tarquiniensis,* the entrance was less monumental and at curfew they closed the gates of the city to isolate it from the countryside. In the surroundings of a necropolis you can never take too many precautions. Is this sensible habit still observed? Apparently not. At the barrier of San Giusto, the main entrance to Tarquinia, we found no trace of a gate.

At the Palazzo Vitelleschi, which holds the Etruscan Museum (this palace has the arrogant look of a historical building and an access ramp for mules), they tell us that the custodian is at the tombs with a Dutch painter, who is making copies in the Tomb of the Lionesses. We go back along the Corso Vittorio Emanuele and seek out the noblemen's club with its little wrought-iron terrace, which at this hour is deserted since it is the hour of Pan, the most silent and solitary. But last time it was the hour of the promenade, and the club members crowded the tiny balcony like huge quails, giant wading birds, calves packed into an iron cage; while others stood below, in front of the doorway, and flirted with the girls who were trooping up and down the street, holding hands, calling out to each other, and tittering with little nervous laughs. One of these members, not one of the aerial ones but one of the earthbound, was introduced to us by Cardarelli as a "great hunter, great drinker, and great lover in the sight of God."

We leave by the Porta Tarquinia and linger on the road for Vetralla. In this same place, the previous time, we met a cart on which a girl lay looking at the sky and softly raving. We asked a man following the cart what was the matter with her, and he told us that the poor girl had been bitten by a tarantula. A diplomatic reply. Among the ancient ghosts circulating in these parts, there must be some that are famished and even a few who bite and cause delirium.

This countryside has the face of an old woman and is traversed by a papal aqueduct as by an enormous worm.

Here is how Dante, with his usual pessimism, describes these places:

> *Non han si aspri sterpi, né si folti*
> *quelle fiere selvagge, che in odio hanno*
> *tra Cecina e Corneto i luoghi colti.*

> (The wild beasts that hate
> the cultivated places between Cecina and
> Corneto have not such harsh or dense thickets.)

The bad moods of poets should not be taken literally, nor even their good moods. Very often it is nothing but a superficial color, which the poet chooses rather than some other, considering it more expressive and effective. But the poet's mind is not in question, nor his judgment, and still less his intelligence. If this last is strong and deep, it remains as motionless and colorless as water.

People around here call the area of the Tarquinia necropolis Monterozzi, from the tumuli that dot the terrain with so many *monterozzi*, or mounds. Our cry of "Tomb keeper!" goes unanswered. The land hereabouts is as deserted as the sea. The existence of the tombs is revealed only by the little doorways that stick up from the ground like the hatches on the deck of a ship, but all of them, mute and impenetrable, are closed with iron gates and padlocks. One last time the cry "Tomb keeper!" hopelessly leaves us, and falls in the distance, between the legs of the aqueduct, like a dead bird.

When Italy was still divided and some of its sons went seeking their fortune outside its territory, a strange type of Italian, a combination of the adventurous and the chivalrous, Marco Polo and Garibaldi, used to go traveling about the world. Minus the British phlegm and some knowledge of physics and mechanics, he was the Latin equivalent of the Cyrus Smiths, Phileas Foggs, and other Anglo-Saxon heroes of the saga sung by Jules Verne. We who by chance spent our childhood in the harsh valleys of Thessaly, where our father, with a cork helmet on his head and a sweaty bandanna around his neck, laid the tracks for the railroad, had occasion to meet more than one of these cordial and ingenuous soldiers of fortune. But we have a happy memory of one in particular, whose name was Pistono and who had as many talents as Ulysses. He did little engineering jobs, although he had no training or diploma, he gave lessons "about things" to us children, he organized fireworks displays for the birthday of the king of Italy, and for the same occasion composed odes in homage to the female members of the royal family:

> The elect triad
> of Graces is complete:
> Jolanda and Elena,
> the devout Margherita. . . .

He dedicated laudatory poems to our father, "pioneer of civilization":

> Now rise palaces,
> now rise gardens,
> where before there was nothing
> but a forest of pines.

Whom do we find after all these years on the doorstep of the Palazzo Vitelleschi, where he had been waiting for us, having learned of our arrival in Tarquinia and having been unable to find us in the area of the tombs? It is Pistono, our good-natured guide, who took us on educational walks at the foot of Mount Pelion or along the banks of the Peneus and taught us the qualities of plants and their properties, who was able to imitate the voices of birds so well that the very blackbirds came up to him, cocking at him in profile one round and astonished eye; who played "fire games" for our enjoyment, scattering gunpowder on the ground in the shape of a wheel or snake or flower and igniting it in a fearful burst. Having been our guide in the fabled world of childhood, it was only right that Pistono should also guide us in the deep abodes of the Etruscan dead.

Enrico Rastelli, keeper of the tombs of Tarquinia, he who is for us the reincarnation of the good mentor of our childhood, is waiting for us with the bunch of keys in his left hand, the acetylene lamp in his right, and a handkerchief arranged tightly on his head with four knots at the corners, to protect him from the sun.

It is not advisable to visit the Etruscan tombs alone, and we, having already suffered such a harsh blow by spraining our left ankle in front of the Tomb of the Tarquins in Cerveteri, have asked Dora to accompany us in Tarquinia. And Dora takes us by the elbow in descending the stairs, guides our steps across the slippery floor of the mortuary rooms, and is for us in visiting these hypogea what Antigone was for blind Oedipus on the journey from Thebes to Colonus.

The stairs in the tombs of Tarquinia can be divided into original and restored. Those that have been restored are not beautiful but they are safe. But when the stairway is original, that is to say, worn out, full of holes, and very steep, the descent becomes an attraction in an amusement park.

In place of eyes Dora has two little balls of multicolored glass, and if we were still children, we would ask her to lend them to us to play marbles. She takes notes for us of erudite documentation, and in addition to Antigone, she is the Henriette to our Renan. We ask her to make a note on the painted head of a girl of the Velcha family in the Tomb of the Ogre (4th century B.C.), which is reproduced in a three-color plate in the Treccani Encyclopaedia. This girl is seen in profile, her head wreathed, her hair gathered like the stern of a ship in a net on the back of her neck, her upper lip curled in an attitude of "Greek" scorn. But when we examine Dora's notes, we find that she has written Treccani as "3 Cani" [3 Dogs].

Giambattista Vico was right. The etymological sense reveals the persistence in man of his sense of origins. All the more, therefore, in woman, whose soul is so much fresher than man's and closer to original things. A sister-in-law of ours, attractive and full of high spirits, calls the Balearics "balnearic islands," since it seems right to her that an island should reveal its qualities in its name as well. Napoleon changed *rentes viagères* into *rentes voyagères,* and the idea of a "traveling" annuity probably satisfied in him that curiosity we all nourish, to explain to ourselves the hidden significance of words.

Once again our attention is caught by the fortuitous play of chance. Serious people don't bother with these things, but we are not serious people. The Greeks too were highly attentive to words heard by chance, and to certain bodily sensations that they interpreted as omens: buzzing in the ears, itching palms, twitching eyelids.

This time the "game" is started by Enrico Rastelli, who inserts a large key into the iron door of a tomb among the "new excavations," and announces that this is the *Tomb of the Baron.*

The absurd image of an Etruscan baron takes shape in one's mind. Absurd images are the most seductive. Not because we are attracted by the unnatural, but by optimism and the need for activity. Not all, but some few of us are composed of will and ambition; we do not consider people and things unless they are "dependent" on us. What is already logical in itself, self-contained, *does not interest us.* Love, in its active form, is our optimistic, generous, Christian ambition to give to others what those others lack. May the beloved woman take care always to preserve "something she lacks." Her perfection would make our love pointless. The image of the Etruscan baron, so unlikely at first, little by little becomes acceptable, and even familiar. This new type of Etruscan was attractive, produced by a monstrous combination of the Etruscan man with the medieval baron in his iron harness, the Sicilian baron of Verga's novels, and the Baltic baron of the generation of the Hindenburgs. We love the infinite possibilities of fantasy, this poetic liberation. Children ought to be brought up in a way that favors the development, not the atrophy, of the imaginative faculty.

"It's called the *Tomb of the Baron,*" says Enrico Rastelli, starting down the dark staircase ahead of us and thrusting into the darkness the stinking burner of his acetylene lamp, "because it was discovered in 1829 by the German Baron Kestner."

Enrico Rastelli has destroyed our illusions.

Pistono was more prudent. He alone knew how to treat children. And grownups as well.

Tarquinia, 5 September

We ask the reader to pardon us for this long digression, and before leading him to the end of this journey through that part of Italy most rich in the arcane, we promise to give him a detailed and exhaustive description of the necropolis of Tarquinia. If we have any ambition, it is of a precise and bureaucratic kind. But is the reader perhaps opposed to digressions? Does he believe in a goal not only for ordinary life, but literary life as well? Is he longing for a story with a beginning and end? This is contrary to the noble purpose of literature, which knows neither beginning nor end, and wants only to give form and shimmer to the continuous present in life. Let the reader beware and not allow himself to be distracted from the art of strolling. "Seriousness" is much different from what he may think.

The Tomb of Hunting and Fishing awakens memories in us of a previous life, when men and beasts lived in friendly community. Pythagoras, that Keyserling of antiquity, must have felt equally disturbed when he recognized in the Temple of Apollo in Delphi, and in the form of a votive offering, the weapons he had borne as Euphorbus, when he had fought for the defense of Troy and been slain by Menelaus. One of the most profound passages in the *Iliad* is the sudden speech that erupts from the foaming, rosy lips of Achilles' horse Xanthus, and the forecast that the eloquent quadruped gives to his master of his approaching death and the best way to celebrate it. Homer spoke well because the time when life was a living fable was still fresh in his mind. But little by little memory becomes clouded in the animalists and fades, although in each of them remains, along with the final recollection, the last trace of a mysterious resemblance as well. Aesop was a hunchback because he too was a bit of a dromedary. La Fontaine, with his long pointed nose, was himself somewhat of a stork; and on the forehead of our own Trilussa, the tight stubbornness of the ram reappears once more, when his huge, delicate hands stroke in the air the neck and flanks of the invisible animals, gazelles, bitterns, or piglets, that whisper their secrets in his ear.

In the Tomb of Hunting and Fishing, the horses do not speak, they laugh, at some joke perhaps daring twenty-five centuries ago but still fresh. Who did speak? Certainly not this hare walking at the head of a procession of hunters who return from the chase with their dogs and horses; the hare is incapable of making you laugh, fearful as it is and preoccupied with itself; but probably this horse, disguised as a vegetable, and showing off its green coat here close by. The Etruscan painters worked before the invention of verismo, and they knew how to paint with a light hand on thin plaster, like someone who turns a squinting eye to the sky and writes according to the flight of his imagination. If the horses in the Tomb of Hunting and Fishing are green, the trees in compensation are blue.

The boats in the fishing section carry on their prows a splendid brown eye against the evil eye, and the fisherman standing in the stern handles a single oar like a gondolier. Jellyfish rise from the depths of the sea and little prawn-shaped men dive from above, both rendered with a simplification of form that anticipates the painting of Paul Klee. But where are the modern painters?

The same tomb, in order to consume all the fish and game on display, depicts a banquet at which women act as "seats" for the guests. It is an unexpected sight. We knew that you could stand on principles, but that you could also sit on women we had yet to learn. Not to mention the discomfort and the absence of the first quality of every seat, which is to be cool. But here there is obviously some error. True, in this same Tarquinia a few years ago, we sat at a hospitable table, and the *despoina,* or *domina,* or lady of the house served us *fettuccine alla chitarra, ossibuchi,* and quantities of cheese and fruit, but when we begged her to sit down with us at the table, she frantically refused. We have, however, called the Etruscans "our romantic fathers"; we know that in them spirit triumphed over matter, and we also know that where the spirit flourishes feminism flourishes too. The "degradation of women," which some would like to take for austerity of customs and a tradition of ancient wisdom, is simply a question of convenient brutality.

The Tomb of the Augurs is a bold anticipation of

Andrea Sperelli's* *garçonnière.* The painted fabrics on the walls and ceiling give the interior a "candy-box" look. The *gemütlich* quality is obtained through four colors diluted in water. The very doors are not real but painted, and one can easily imagine the tricks played by the Etruscan Sperelli on his Elena Muti: "Would you care to come, milady, into the adjoining bedchamber?" And "milady," fooled by the door painted in *trompe-l'oeil,* runs into the wall and bumps her nose. Add the greater refinement of this Etruscan *garçonnière,* these figures of mimes posing like Serge Lifar, with undulating arms and hands drooping like flowers on their stalks, these scenes of complicated and sadistic wrestling, men fighting with their heads in sacks, dogs participating in the combat and biting where they can, torture collars clamped on necks. What is the connection between Eros, Mars, and Ponos? A friend of ours once bought a pack of postcards in a sealed envelope in Paris, and when he got home and opened the envelope, he found a series of photographs of wrestling champions. The Etruscan Sperelli is much more decadent than d'Annunzio's.

In the Tomb of the Bulls, we find bulls with human and clearly Basedovian features, Uncle Sams with goatees and shaved mustaches, and some characters from our favorite mythology: Priam's son Troilus on horseback, Achilles armed to the teeth and springing swiftly forward out of ambush, two lions reclining at the foot of a fountain, a chimaera that has distributed its

---

*The protagonist of d'Annunzio's novel *Il Piacere,* published in 1889. (Tr.)

heads on the tips of its wings and the end of its tail, in imitation of a microphone placed at the top of a shaft, and a decoration of pomegranates along the molding, so stylized as to look like the sphere of empire surmounted by a cross as seen in official portraits of the king of England.

Having concluded the visit to the front room, our guide invites us to go into the back room, and on a wall where black Lucumons sleep like leeches, he shines the rumbling beam of his acetylene lamp. We close our eyes for fear of having seen incorrectly, but when we re-open them we have to admit that we have not been deceived. The scene is one of such obscenity that the painter himself took fright and left it unfinished. We are to the left, to the right is the custodian, and between him and us is Dora, our collaborator with the multicolored eyes. No one speaks, and all three of us stand still in a serious and natural manner. But after a few moments a great sadness descends on us, an infinite dismay. Where were Menander's wits when he combined love and death? Death has no brothers, but only a sister: obscenity. We go back up into the light, talking seriously of one thing or another. Our collaborator is admirable in her sense of duty. Before leaving, she asks if she should write down anything in her notebook. But without looking at us.

In the unfinished part of that painting, the figuration has remained scratched on the wall: a sign of how precise was the technique of the Etruscan fresco painters. The women with their cone-shaped hairdos look like so many ears of corn, and yet even in them, our incurable quixotism has made us see so many saints.

Literature and art lose their way partly by abandoning fixed forms. Every time a novelist mentions a character, he tacks onto him a different adjective. For Homer, on the other hand, Hera is always *boòpis,* Io always *rododattila,* and Odysseus is always *polütlas* or *polümetis.* The type is fixed once and for all. This is a convenience for both writer and reader. We find an equal fixing of types in the Etruscan painters. Great painting, prior to the invention of Impressionism and Expressionism, has its alphabet. In Etruscan paintings, animals always face forward, and men always have their heads in profile and the eye facing forward. Always. The determination of type is also indicated by the colors: the bodies of men are red, those of women white. In the back room of the Tomb of the Bulls, we found a third type: the pink man. Why has this useful distinction been abandoned? Infinite mistakes would be avoided, vast amounts of ambiguity.

In the Tomb of the Ogre, more recent in time, the architecture is richer, the painting more knowing: eyes are seen in profile in the faces in profile, and together with naturalism, decadence also begins. The very plaster has been prepared more carefully under the overly bright painting, and the ceiling is coffered as in the Basilica of Maxentius. Moral content also enters into these frescoes. The passage from evil to good is expressed by this dead man led by a psychopomp who is no longer the horrible Charun nor the horrendous Tuchulcha, but an indifferent and beautiful genius, an androgynous Thanatos, brother of gentle Sleep. Life's progress toward perfection gradually erases singularities of character, and disparities of sex, passion, and desire; it removes expression even from the gaze, and arrives at a blank, colorless, highly transparent form. The journey of the intelligence is about to end.

From the height on which stands the Tomb of the Lionesses, one can see the hill on whose top the Etruscan Tarquinia was built. It is an old man's bald head that goes on thinking. At its feet runs the Marta river, which comes from Bolsena and empties into the Tyrrhenian Sea, near Porto Clementino where convicts toil under the sun building pyramids of salt. The port of the Etruscans was called Gravisca but has disappeared. To our left is the Montagna della Tolfa, and this sea before us is too deserted, too bleak, to let us hope for the arrival of an Isolde. And anyway what's the use? The only friend around here is death.

Rastelli slings the bunch of keys across his back and starts down the slope. Formerly when Rastelli accompanied tourists into the hypogea, he would leave his keys at the entrance to be guarded by Fritz, the intelligent and faithful Pomeranian. But Fritz is no more and the one consolation left to Rastelli is to remember that D. H. Lawrence mentioned the dog in his *Etruscan Places*. When Rastelli is sad, he opens Lawrence's book and looks at the page that speaks of Fritz. But what, oh what, does that page say? Rastelli will never know, because it is written in English.

It is noon, which is midnight for the dead. The hatches of the tombs open one by one, and all our new and cherished friends appear on the thresholds: the Etruscan baron, the Andrea Sperelli of the fifth century B.C., the pink men, the women with cornstalks in their hair, the laughing horses, all of them. Some stay on the ground, others rise like balloons, and all of them together make up an inscription in which, more by intuition than knowledge, we read: "Why are you leaving? War is thundering over the world. Stay with us and all will go well for you."

What should we do? Go back among the living? Or heed the advice of the Etruscan dead?

Tarquinia, 6 September

In the paintings in the Tomb of the Ogre, the most advanced of the Tarquinia necropolis, Greek characters mingle with ones from Etruscan mythology. There is greater affinity between Etruscans and Greeks than between Greeks and Romans, and this is probably determined by the fact that there is romantic sentiment in the Greeks but not in the Romans. Tuchulcha stands with his horrendous snout between Theseus and Pirithous, the first seated and beautiful, the second reduced by time and saltpeter to less than a shadow. Next to the group of Agamemnon and Tiresias is a painted tree with many little red men running up and down the branches.

The surrealist mechanism is easy to use and within reach of everyone, including women and children. Children indeed are surrealists by nature. As a mechanism it rather resembles that of humor. It is a matter of creating an emotion by combining two things that by their nature do not go together. The bird in the tree is real; the man in the tree is surreal.

The surrealist vein has existed since the world began, and so it was also there in the time of the Etruscan painters. Why is there so much hostility to the Surrealism of today, and such indulgent acceptance of the surrealism of the third century B.C.?

A few evenings ago, a newsreel showed us some of the rooms in the new Baghdad museum, and while the voice of the announcer lauded the "powerful realism" of Assyro-Babylonian sculpture, magnificent winged lions with human heads and Smith Brothers beards paraded across the screen. Is the newsreel announcer truly convinced of what he so confidently asserts?

The subject of men in trees was taken up again after 2229 years and brought to perfection by a young Italian artist named Titino delle Fornaci. He arrived in Paris when Surrealism was all the rage, and thinking that glory would not smile on him unless he too was attuned to the time, he began to paint fish roosting in trees. But all the same, glory did not smile on him.

The man in the tree has the characteristics of a Freudian theme. Freud is dead, and here in Italy we have heard all kinds of things about him. Catholic by nature, the Italian is opposed to anything that undermines man as God's repository and tries to draw out the truth about man. Is this the reason why there is so little psychology in Italy, why there are so few novels? For us, Freud, after Schopenhauer, is the best of educators. Even the grave, tranquil pace of his prose is the pace of an educator. Freud shows us the things of life, "all" the things, even the most hidden, but he does not judge them: he leaves the pupil free to accept them or not. To educate, as the word says, should only mean "to guide."

Some twenty years ago, three friends were coming out of the house of Armando Spadini at Villetta Parioli around midnight, and took the direction of Via Flaminia. One of them was the author of these pages. The countryside was deserted and moonlit. As they were about to enter the Arco Oscuro, the three friends saw in the middle of the Arco a nude woman in the pose of a statue, her arms uplifted and her head held high. Her body glowed in the shadows. When they had got over their astonishment, the three friends, hugging the wall, passed through the arch in front of the naked woman, who gave no sign that she saw them. Coming out the other side toward the Villa Giulia, they went on their way, talking about the strange encounter. But all of a sudden, and not behind them as might have been expected, but in front, they heard a female voice singing a raucous song in words of a Nordic language, and a few moments later, on the fork of a tree at the edge of the road, they saw the same naked woman in the same pose of a statue, singing under the moon.

A few days later, the author of these pages discovered the woman of the Arco Oscuro and the tree in the house of friends. She was covered by a very high-necked dress and was engaged in delicately kissing the rim of a teacup. He asked to be introduced to her, and after they had talked for a while, he reminded her of that nocturnal encounter. The lady lowered her eyes and replied, "Yes, it was I, but needless to say, I was living one of my paintings." She was a Scandinavian artist, and in her paintings almost always treated the subject of naked men in trees. What would happen if all painters set out to "live" the subjects of their paintings in public?

The beard of Agamemnon, who stands talking with

Tiresias next to the tree of the little men, is of that lovely deep blue that the sea takes on around noon, when a light west wind rises. Deep blue beards were very common in painted sculpture (all statues were painted before the spiritualist concept that "art expresses the inexpressible"), and the blue beard was probably the "ideal" of black beards (cf. hair "with deep blue reflections").

Someone to whom we showed a still life of pears that we had painted in deep blue monochrome exclaimed, "Blue pears don't exist!" and was ready to weep with rage. In his opinion, those blue pears were an offense to reality. We wanted to put to him the famous question "Is nature real?" but remembered in time how irritable he was. We direct the question to our readers, who we hope are less splenetic, and we urge them to let us know where reality begins and where it ends. Not even Ivan the Terrible would be so cruel as to expel the color-blind from reality, and what are we to say of that reality discovered through infrared and ultraviolet radiations, which for man is only perceptible with the help of special sensitive plates, but which some insects, such as ants, see with the naked eye? Painters of Italy, if you do not want to be less than the ants, paint blue pears and beards of the same color.

Formicola (ant) is a Tuscan form of *formica,* and even Collodi uses it in *Pinocchio.* To us, *formicola* sounds more spirited than *formica,* as well as more expressive of the act of *formicolare* (swarming). One ought to compose a small dictionary of only flavorful words, for use in childhood and for adults who preserve childish, that is to say straightforward, tastes: *formicola* for *formica, carciofani* for *carciofi* (artichokes), *bericòcole* for *albicocche* (apricots). Not to be confused, however — God forbid! — with d'Annunzian synonyms: *veltro* for *levriero* (greyhound), *navarca* for admiral or sea captain, *àlluce* for big toe.

Whence comes the urge to go back to living in trees? In addition to a lacustrine age, men must also have gone through an arboreal one. And the memory of it survives in some of them. Tree life is still common among savages. (We recommend in this regard an excellent book by Jules Verne: *Le Village aérien.*) Anyway savages gradually collect what civilized men throw away. One day the radio will be used only by savages. And on that day, let me tell you . . .

Besides the paintings already mentioned, we find in the Tomb of the Ogre a Geryon with three heads, all of them in profile, and wearing armor that looks as though it had been painted by Rembrandt; a Proserpina in whom Botticelli and the "spiritual" maidens of the Pre-Raphaelites emerge; and a Pluto with a wolf's-head helmet, anticipating Michelangelo's *Pensieroso.*

The approximation method is deplorable — like saying "Munich, the Athens of Germany" or "De Amicis, the Italian Dickens" — and we apologize for having used it ourselves, but it is sometimes useful in showing the poverty of the world and the tenacity of certain forms of stupidity.

The most interesting painting in the Tomb of the Ogre is *Ulysses and Polyphemus.* This painting is all the more interesting in that it requires an effort at discovery, like certain puzzles whose caption reads: "Here is the forest, now find the three-masted schooner." We stood in front of *Ulysses and Polyphemus* for some time, I, the tomb keeper Enrico Rastelli, and Dora, our collaborator with the multicolored eyes, and the three of us unanimously declared that despite the ravages of time, the painting of Ulysses and Polyphemus was completely clear. But when Dora, in support of her statement, pointed her painted fingernail at the eye of the Cyclops, into which the man who said his name was "Nobody" was about to drive a stake, it turned out on closer examination that what Dora had mistaken for the eye of the Cyclops was instead Mister Nobody's right foot. If you carefully compare the texts of art critics with the works they are expounding, you will very often find feet in place of eyes.

A frightful hole gapes near the painting of Ulysses and Polyphemus, and leads back into darkness. Unless you perform effective and timely exorcisms, you may well see Charun, the dreadful psychopomp, and Tuchulcha with two boar's tusks sticking out of his mouth like the Kaiser's mustaches, emerge from that hole. The hole is a leftover from the dangerous soundings that were originally made, before the more rational method of excavation now in use, and which consists in delicately probing all around the tumulus until the stairway is found that leads down into the tomb. There was a time when they broke open the tumulus at any point, and descended into it willy-nilly, smashing everything along the way, whether architecture or painting. If the paintings in the Tomb of the Ogre are in good shape, it is thanks to the star that protects the Etruscan painters and us who love them.

At the entrance to the Tomb of the Ogre, we notice a basin full of human bones. We ask Enrico Rastelli and he tells us that they are "apocryphal bones." This is how poetry is unexpectedly born. The attribution of the *Apocalypse* is still uncertain: why not attribute it to Enrico Rastelli, keeper of the tombs of Tarquinia? Among these bones we recognize a few brainpans, some of them smaller, others bigger. "The smaller ones are women," says Rastelli, who is evidently not a feminist.

The excavations of the necropolis of Tarquinia are at present at a standstill; excavation of the nearby Etruscan city, however, is going full blast. The first trophies extracted from Bald Mountain (we speak advisedly: up here echo the grave and solitary tones of Mussorgsky) have already traveled the road to the Vitelleschi museum, with two winged horses in terracotta leading the march.

Before leaving the capital of our Romantic Fathers, we enter the Tarquinia museum and see the relief of the two winged horses displayed on an easel. They are magnificent, but you don't know whom to admire more, the ancient artist or the modern restorer.

Our eye is caught, in an adjacent room, by some paintings that are clearly not Etruscan. It is a small exhibition of local artists; on the center wall hangs a picture entitled *The Cordial.* It shows an old man suddenly taken ill and surrounded by his family, including his wife who hands him a small glass.

We are curious to know whether in the year 4378, after a number of years equal to that which separates us from the time when Etruscan artists were painting the tombs of Tarquinia, we will return here in an advanced period of metempsychosis and again see *The Cordial,* placed on an easel and carefully restored.

Whoever is alive will see.

*"What? You bring me to visit your country, you give me a glimpse of how much good, how much peace, how much dignity there is in these houses that look empty and instead are . . . (*spes mortuum: l'espoir des morts*), and now you abandon me?"*

Charun replies:

"What have you done to deserve a remission of your sentence? It's up to you to keep working, toiling."

"Charun, take me with you!"

Charun does not listen to me. He goes away. He disappears like light extinguished in the light.

And to stay on, and on, and on . . .